Today v

Today with Amos, Hosea and Micah

Clifford Hill

All rights reserved

No part of this publication may be reproduced, stored in a retrieval system, or transmitted in any form by any means, electronic, mechanical, photocopying, recording or otherwise, without the prior permission of The Handsel Press Ltd

British Library Cataloguing in Publication Data:
a catalogue record for this publication
is available from the British Library

ISBN 978-1-912052-91-2

© **Clifford Hill 2025**

The right of Clifford Hill to be identified
as the author of this work has been asserted by him
in accordance with the Copyright, Designs and Patents Act 1988

Typeset in 10.5pt Minion Pro at Haddington, Scotland

Printed by Bell and Bain, Glasgow

Cover image by Anthony Whelan

CONTENTS

FOREWORD BY TOM LENNIE		6
INTRODUCING THE EIGHTH CENTURY BC PROPHETS		8
TABLE OF EVENTS		12
INTRODUCTION TO *TODAY WITH AMOS*		14
1	THE WORDS OF AMOS Amos 1:1	18
2	THE LORD ROARS Amos 1:2	20
3	JUDGEMENT ON DAMASCUS Amos 1:3-5	22
4	JUDGEMENT ON THE PHILISTINES Amos 1:6-10	24
5	JUDGEMENT UPON EDOM AND AMMON Amos 1:11-15	26
6	JUDGEMENT UPON MOAB AND JUDAH Amos 2:1-5	28
7	JUDGEMENT ON ISRAEL Amos 2:6-16	30
8	JUDGEMENT ON THE CHOSEN ONES Amos 3:1-8	32
9	THE MESSAGE OF WARNING Amos 3:9-15	34
10	WARNING TO THE WOMEN Amos 4:1-3	36
11	SACRIFICES AND FREEWILL OFFERINGS Amos 4:4-5	38
12	WARNINGS IGNORED Amos 4:6-11	40
13	PREPARE TO MEET GOD Amos 4:12-13	42
14	A LAMENT FOR ISRAEL Amos 5:1-17	44
15	THE DAY OF THE LORD Amos 5:18-20	46
16	RELIGIOUS SACERDOTALISM Amos 5:21-27	48
17	FALSE COMPLACENCY Amos 6:1-7	50
18	THE PRIDE OF ISRAEL Amos 6:8-14	52
19	LOCUSTS AND FIRE Amos 7:1-6	54
20	THE PLUMB-LINE OF THE LORD Amos 7:7-9	56
21	AMOS AND AMAZIAH Amos 7:10-17	58
22	THE BASKET OF RIPE FRUIT Amos 8:1-6	60

23	THE PRIDE OF JACOB Amos 8:7-14	62
24	A FINAL WARNING OF DESTRUCTION Amos 9:1-8a	64
25	RESTORATION OF ISRAEL Amos 9:8b-15	66
	CONCLUSION – THE UNIQUE MESSAGE OF AMOS	68
	INTRODUCTION TO *TODAY WITH HOSEA*	70
1	HOSEA'S MARRIAGE Hosea 1:1-11	72
2	REUNION AND HOPE Hosea 1:10-2:3	74
3	ISRAEL CALLED TO ACCOUNT Hosea 2:2-17	76
4	A NEW COVENANT RELATIONSHIP Hosea 2: 18-23	78
5	THE REDEMPTION OF GOMER Hosea 3:1-5	80
6	THE CHARGE AGAINST ISRAEL Hosea 4:1-13	82
7	THE DANGERS OF IDOLATRY Hosea 4:14-19	84
8	INEVITABILITY OF JUDGEMENT Hosea 5:1-7	86
9	BATTLE STATIONS Hosea 5:8-15	88
10	UNREPENTANT ISRAEL Hosea 6:1-8	90
11	IMMEDIATE RESTORATION IMPOSSIBLE Hosea 6:9 – 7:7	92
12	ALLIANCES WITH FOREIGN NATIONS Hosea 7:8-16	94
13	REAPING THE WHIRLWIND Hosea 8:1-10	96
14	THE DESTINY OF ISRAEL AND JUDAH Hosea 8: 11-14	98
15	THE FESTIVALS OF GOD Hosea 9:1-9	100
16	GRAPES IN THE DESERT Hosea 9:10-17	102
17	THE CONSEQUENCES OF DISOBEDIENCE Hosea 10:1-11	104
18	BREAK UP UNPLOUGHED GROUND Hosea 10:11-15	106
19	GOD'S LOVE FOR ISRAEL Hosea 11:1-7	108
20	THE DILEMMA FACING GOD Hosea 11:8-11	110
21	THE TREACHERY OF ISRAEL Hosea 11:12 – 12:6	112
22	THE INDICTMENT OF ISRAEL Hosea 12:7-14	114
23	THE LORD'S ANGER AGAINST ISRAEL Hosea 13:1-8	116

24	RANSOM AND REDEMPTION Hosea 13:9-16	118
25	REPENTANCE, SALVATION AND BLESSING Hosea 14:1-9	120
	CONCLUSION – THE UNIQUE MESSAGE OF HOSEA	122
	INTRODUCTION TO *TODAY WITH MICAH*	125
1	MICAH SPEAKS TO THE WORLD Micah 1:1-4	128
2	JUDGEMENT ON SAMARIA Micah 1:5-7	130
3	JUDGEMENT UPON JERUSALEM Micah 1:8-16	132
4	PLANS FOR THE FUTURE Micah 2:1-5	134
5	FALSE PROPHETS Micah 2:6-11	136
6	DELIVERANCE OF THE REMNANT Micah 2:12-13	138
7	UNJUST LEADERS AND JUDGES Micah 3:1-4	140
8	MORE FALSE PROPHECIES Micah 3:5-8	142
9	THE WORD OF THE LORD TO ISRAEL Micah 3:9-12	144
10	THE MOUNTAIN OF THE LORD Micah 4:1-5	146
11	THE WAY OF THE LORD Micah 4:6-10	148
12	THE WAY TO REDEMPTION Micah 4:11 – 5:1	150
13	THE HONOURING OF BETHLEHEM Micah 5:2-5	152
14	THE ASSYRIAN INVASION Micah 5:5-9	154
15	THE COMING DAY OF THE LORD Micah 5:10-15	156
16	THE CASE AGAINST ISRAEL Micah 6:1-5	158
17	THE REQUIREMENTS OF THE LORD Micah 6:6-8	160
18	ISRAEL'S GUILT AND PUNISHMENT Micah 6:9-16	162
19	ISRAEL'S MISERY Micah 7:1-7	164
20	THE HOPE OF THE NATION Micah 7:7-9	166
21	THE LIGHT OF THE WORLD Micah 7:10-13	168
22	THE SHEPHERD AND THE FLOCK Micah 7:14-17	170
23	THE GREAT REDEEMER Micah 7:18-20	172
	CONCLUSION – MICAH'S UNIQUE MESSAGE	174

FOREWORD

Anyone who personally knows Clifford Hill, as I have had the privilege of doing for a number of years, or who has followed the ministry of *Prophecy Today UK* – of which he is the founder – over a period of time, or who has regularly listened to Cliff's bi-monthly '*State of the Nation*' audio messages, will be well aware of his ardent love for the Word of God, and especially the biblical prophets.

Unquestionably, Dr Hill has long been one of Britain's finest scholars of the Old Testament prophets, with a string of published books and booklets on various related topics. These include:

• The formidable 300-page *Prophecy Past and Present* (1989) – an in-depth study of prophecy and the whole area of God's revelation to man which won a publishers 'Book of the Year' award in the USA. The major emphasis was necessarily the Bible, which provides us with the only reliable guide to the nature and purpose of revelation.

• The unique, pioneering study, *Living in Babylon* (2016) – along with its companion volume, *Living Victoriously in Babylon*, both co-written with Monica: a historical study of sixth century BC Judah in exile in Babylon, outlining the transformation of the exilic Jews as a covenant people of God, preparing them for their return to Jerusalem to re-establish the life of the city, to rebuild the Temple and to reconstruct the city walls.

In between these pioneering ventures, Clifford embarked on a three-volume series of devotional studies (1999 to 2002), centred on the Old Testament book of Isaiah, bringing fresh light on the relevance of Isaiah's message for today. During these same years, Dr Hill wrote two volumes of similar devotional commentaries on the book of Jeremiah – perhaps Cliff's 'favourite' Old Testament prophet – carefully explaining both the background and the meaning of the biblical text.

These books form part of the series '*Today with the Prophets*'. More recently, an artfully illustrated two-volume study of Ezekiel was published (2024), and following hot on the heels of those books comes a further volume, this time on the not-so-'minor' prophets Amos, Hosea and Micah.

Following a general introduction to these servants of God, some helpful historical background information is offered on each of them.

Presented in similarly devotional style, *Today with Amos, Hosea and Micah* examines the life and ministry of these three biblical characters in around 24 short chapters each. All of the major themes of these ancient books are discussed, including:

- **Amos:** His judgements on surrounding nations (chapters 1 – 2); Israel's complacency (chapter 6); the plumbline of the Lord (chapter 7); the vision of the basket of ripe fruit (chapter 8); and an account of Israel's restoration (chapter 9).

- **Hosea**: His marriage (chapter 1); the charges against Israel (chapters 2 & 4); Israel's unrepentance (chapter 6); and Israel's ransom and redemption (chapter 13).

- **Micah**: Exposing false prophets (chapters 2 & 3); the mountain of the Lord (chapter 4); the coming day of the Lord (chapter 5); and the great redeemer (chapter 7).

Like the others in the *Today with . . .* series, this book is no dry academic read. Rather, the author's love for the Scriptures, and his earnest desire to enable others to enjoy the fruits of his own discoveries, comes over on every page.

And so it is that I very much welcome this highly readable volume, which will surely serve to enrich believers' knowledge of the word of God and reveal the remarkable ways in which God used ordinary men from nearly 3,000 years ago to speak both judgement and hope to his covenant people.

It's a message that is still highly relevant today.

Tom Lennie
Editor of *Prophecy Today*

INTRODUCTING THE EIGHTH CENTURY BC PROPHETS

Shockwaves of Truth

The first half of the eighth century BC was a time of international peace, economic growth, and domestic tranquility for both Judah and Israel. But by the middle of the century the whole scene was about to erupt into the most challenging half-century in the history of the people of Israel until that date. In fact, it would see the end of the northern kingdom of Israel in 721 BC. Most of the leaders of both Israel and Judah were oblivious of the danger facing them, but four men were given the spiritual insight to blow a trumpet of warning that could have saved Israel from destruction and prepared Judah for the testing times ahead.

Both Israel and Judah were enjoying economic prosperity but were riven by injustice and corruption in their domestic life, and with idolatry and spiritual blindness in their religious practices.

The shockwaves created by the four prophets sent by God would provide a unique revelation of God himself, of his nature and purposes, although they did not succeed in achieving the radical change required in both nations to save them from the disasters foreseen by the prophets. The opening phrase in the ministry of Amos, the first of the writing prophets, sets the tone for the work of all the eighth century BC prophets, **"The Lord roars from Zion and thunders from Jerusalem"** (Amos 1:2).

Many times, 'The Lion of Judah' had roared against the enemies of Israel. Throughout their history since leaving Sinai, the people of Israel had seen Yahweh their God taking the battlefield on their behalf. The Lion of Judah had roared against his enemies. But the roar that Amos hears is quite different as we will see.

The Rechabite Four

The eighth century BC prophets of Israel – Amos, Isaiah, Hosea, and Micah – were firmly within the Rechabite tradition of young men who were set aside by God and anointed by the zeal of Yahweh to withstand the idolatrous practices that were common in the nation and were practised by all classes of society. Their ministry was to call for a return to faith in Yahweh the God of Israel, to denounce idolatry and evil social practices, especially the injustices and oppression exercised by the rich and powerful, and to blow a trumpet of warning of impending judgement upon the land due to the sins of the leaders both secular and religious.

The eighth century BC prophets were the first writing prophets; the first to have followers who would record their words and produce them in a documentary form for preservation. They all came in quite a short period of time during the second half of the eighth century BC – the most crucial period in the history of Israel since the settlement in the land in the time of Joshua. They appeared at a time of radical social change from the nomadic life of sheep farming to the settled agricultural-based life of a developing economic and social system. This produced towns and cities requiring laws and regulations governing its economic business practices, legal system, political and social life.

Agricultural Revolution

The small farmer was particularly at risk in this period. If, through adverse weather or other factors, he had a poor harvest, in order to survive he might have to borrow money from a wealthy merchant. The time of repayment of the loan would inevitably come and if he could not meet the demand, he only had his land and his labour as security. The land would then be acquired by the merchant who would take large quantities of grain, forcing further borrowing which is denounced in Amos 5:11, *"You trample on the poor and force him to give you grain."* This might reduce the small farmer to slavery, but it was only allowed for a maximum of six years and on the seventh year he had to be set free or choose to remain in slavery for the rest of his life in accordance with regulations set out in Exodus 21:2f.

If the poor man went to court, he got no justice because the rich man had bribed the judge, as Amos says, *"You oppress the righteous and take bribes and you deprive the poor of justice in the courts"* (Am 5:12). A small gift to the judge was sufficient to secure the wealthy man's triumph in the law court – so a poor man was reduced to slavery for *"a pair of sandals"* (Am 2:6). Micah, similarly, denounced the oppression of the small farmer by the wealthy. *"They covet fields and seize them, and houses, and take them. They defraud a man of his home, a fellow man of his inheritance"* (Mic 2:2).

The wealthy landowners were intent on acquiring more land and depriving the poor small farmer of his rights – a practice that was roundly denounced by Isaiah, *"Woe to you who add house to house and join field to field till no space is left and you live alone in the land"* (Isa 5:8). This was all part of the social revolution that was taking place in eighth century BC Israel and Judah. Similar things happened in Britain during the Industrial Revolution when the 'Enclosures Acts' deprived the poor of their traditional grazing rights on open land, driving them off the land into the new urban industrial cities where they became the new landless poor with only their labour to sell.

Plight of the Poor

In Israel and Judah, preachers in the official centres of religion such as Jerusalem and Bethel, like the English bishops centuries later, showed no concern for the poor. They were not interested in matters of social justice in Israel. Their concern was with the religious rules and regulations or 'cultic practices', such as the observance of feasts and festivals together with their regular duties such as making decisions on the eligibility of personal sacrifices. This left the rest of humanity to get on with their lives with no input from the priests. Corruption in high society, cheating in the marketplace, perjury in the law courts, produced self-indulgent luxury on the one hand and grinding poverty and suffering among the poor on the other hand.

These were the conditions that gave rise to the eighth century BC prophets of both Israel and Judah. The official religion of centres such as Jerusalem, Bethel, Gilgal, Beersheba, and the shrines up in the hills offered no redress to the poor or guidance to the leaders of the nation. In all these centres, the religious practices were mainly versions of syncretism in which Yahwism was mixed with the local Baal of the Canaanite shrines and produced a kind of folk religion that satisfied the needs of the wealthy but did not disturb the lives of those who held power in the land. This produced the outward prosperity widely enjoyed by the ruling elite with little or no concern for social morality on a national level or righteousness on an individual basis.

Impact of the Prophets

Into this maelstrom of injustice, prosperity, suffering, and luxury, the Hebrew prophets burst upon the scene. They stood in the tradition of the Rechabites and Nazirites, and the early Nebiim (seers) such as Samuel, Elijah and Micaiah who were from a newly developing agricultural society. Amos came from a shepherding background reflecting the traditional culture of Israel from the time of Moses and the early days of the settlement in the land of Canaan. They were men of immense personal courage actually putting their lives at risk in declaring their message.

Amos, as the first to break upon the tranquil scene, was viewed as a type of social revolutionary denouncing modern civilisation and calling for a return to the simple nomadic days. But his message was much more than that. It was a call from God in fulfilment of his covenant promises, as we will see when we examine the text.

Amos and his successors offered no alternative social system to the Yahwism of Deuteronomy. Their concern was with the injustice they saw around them, and they denounced the elaborate ritual of religion that had become a substitute for the worship of Yahweh. *"'The multitude of your sacrifices – what are they to me?' says the Lord. 'I have more than enough of your burnt offerings'"* (Is 1:11). Religion had become routine, instead of a living faith in the Lord God of Israel.

Recognition of God

What the prophets were seeking was a recognition of Yahweh as the true God who had chosen the people of Israel to be in a covenant relationship. The eighth century BC prophets of Israel revealed the ethical character of the one true God who was the God of Nature, the Creator of the Universe, who held the nations in his hands as the Lord of History. He was not a capricious being like the idols of paganism, but he was a moral God whose nature and principles were timeless and unchangeable, and whose truth should be applied to the changing social order to give vision, permanence, stability, and justice for all of humanity.

Table of Events in the Eighth Century BC reflecting the

PROPHETS OF ISRAEL & JUDAH	KINGDOM OF JUDAH (south)
AMOS	**UZZIAH (786 – 744)**
He came from Tekoa in Judah and ministered in Israel – in Bethel and Samaria. His short ministry began in the last years of Jeroboam II.	He became a leper near the end of his life and had to live in isolation, being banned from the temple.
ISAIAH OF JERUSALEM	**JOTHAM (744 – 735)**
He had a long ministry beginning in the last days of Uzziah, who died in 744 BC, through to the reign of Hezekiah who died in 687. He is the longest serving prophet of the 8th c, beginning around 750, and ending in the early 7th c.	He was put under pressure by both Israel and Syria to join in an alliance against the Assyrians. He died before anything was agreed, and it was left to his 20-year old son Ahaz to deal with the issue.
HOSEA	**AHAZ (735 – 725)**
He was a northerner who began his ministry during the reign of Jeroboam II who died in 744 BC. Hosea was probably active throughout most of the second half of the eighth century BC.	He refused to join the alliance and was attacked, but he appealed to the Assyrians for help. He signed a pact with Tiglath-Pileser and constructed an altar to one of the gods of Assyria in the Jerusalem temple. He was heavily into idolatry and even indulged in human sacrifice – burning his own son.
MICAH	**HEZEKIAH (725 – 687)**
He had a long ministry covering much the same period as Isaiah. He, like Isaiah, was based in Jerusalem but was widely travelled giving him a good knowledge of social and spiritual conditions in both Israel and Judah.	He reversed the idolatrous practices of his father Ahaz and removed the high places from the countryside. He removed altars to foreign gods from the temple; he renounced an alliance with the Assyrians who then began an invasion. When they were attacking Lachish, Hezekiah sent a message seeking peace and offering large amounts of treasure from the Royal household and the temple. Later the Assyrians again invaded and laid seige to Jerusalem. Hezekiah and the prophet Isaiah interceded for Jerusalem, and a plague destroyed the Assyrian army.

Historical Background to the Books of Amos, Hosea & Micah

NORTHERN KINGDOM OF ISRAEL	ASSYRIA – A COMMON ENEMY
JEROBOAM II (786 – 746) Peace and prosperity throughout his forty-year reign, but he was heavily into idolatry and actually established a cultic shrine with an Asherah pole in Samaria. **ZECHARIAH (746 – 745)** Murdered after a six-month reign.	Assyria had a series of internal leadership problems which kept their attention on domestic affairs throughout the first half of the 8th century. Egypt was also quiet, and Babyon had not yet established foreign policy ambitions, meaning a period of peace and prosperity for Israel and Judah.
SHALLUM (745 BC) He was assassinated after one month. **MENAHEM (745 – 738)** He accepted Assyrian sovereignty and paid a heavy tribute.	**TIGLATH-PILESER (745 – 727)** He had ambitions to extend Assyria's borders to the Mediterranean. In 732 Ahaz appealed to Assyria for assistance against Israel. Assyria responded by subdugating Israel, conquering Damascus (Syria) and Philistia – the other two nations in alliance with Israel.
PEKAHIAH (738 – 737) He was assassinated. **PEKAH (737 – 732)** He renounced a treaty with Assyria and established an alliance against the Assyrians, attacking Judah who refused to join him.	**SHALMANESER V (727 – 722)** Conquered Israel and Samaria. Laid siege to Samaria for three years.
HOSHEA (732 – 724) He murdered Pekah and surrendered to the Assyrians. On the death of Shalmaneser he rebelled again. This led to an Assyrian invasion by Sargon who destroyed Samaria in 722/1 – the end of the northern kingdom of Israel.	**SARGON II (722 – 705)** He destroyed Samaria in 722/1, reducing Israel to a province of the Assyrian Empire, and dispersed the population of Israel to settlements around the Assyrian Empire. **SENNACHERIB (705 – 681)** He invaded Judah in 701 BC, laying siege to Jerusalem which resulted in the loss of most of his army.

INTRODUCTION TO *TODAY WITH AMOS*

The Identity of Amos

We know very little about the Prophet Amos, we do not even know his father's name. The name Amos means 'burden' – it comes from the Hebrew verb *amas,* meaning loading a burden upon an animal, which may have been given to Amos in mockery.

The only thing we know about Amos is that he lived in Tekoa (about 10 miles south of Jerusalem), an important city that had been fortified by Rehoboam, the son of Solomon, after Jeroboam's revolution that had formed the northern kingdom of Israel with its capital at Samaria.

Amos' own testimony was, *"I was neither a prophet nor a prophet's son, but I was a shepherd"* (Amos 7:14). The Hebrew word here, translated 'shepherd' is only used in one other place in the Bible – 2 Kings 3:4, which says, *"Now Mesha king of Moab raised sheep."* Clearly Mesha was no ordinary shepherd because the rest of that verse tells us that he had to supply the king of Israel with 100,000 lambs, plus their wool (Amos 7:14). This has led to speculation that Amos was a substantial farmer – a breeder of sheep with a large estate under his control. Even his statement that he also took care of sycamore trees has led to the view that he was not just an ordinary shepherd, but a well-educated man exercising authority over an estate.

Clearly Amos had a good knowledge of the history of Israel and the surrounding nations. This has led scholars to believe that Amos was an important man having contact with travelling merchants from other parts of the region as well as having the time to study the history of his own people.

Historical Background

Amos is the first of the eighth century BC prophets of Israel, appearing in Israel about the middle of the century, 750 BC. The opening words of Amos simply tell us that his ministry was during the reign of king Uzziah of Judah and Jeroboam II king of Israel. It also tells us that this was two years before the earthquake, but where the earthquake happened and when it happened – no one knows.

There is some evidence of an earthquake in northern Israel in the middle of the eighth century BC, but the evidence is not sufficiently strong to give a firm date. The area around Hazor is a possible location as there was considerable destruction there about 750 BC when stones fell in all directions which usually indicates an earthquake.

There are disagreements among biblical scholars over these dates as very little is known about the history of both Israel and Judah from 780 – 740 BC. We do know that it was a time of wider peace, with both Egypt and Assyria going through times of domestic change or facing external challenge. This had allowed international trade to flourish from which Israel had benefited allowing the growth of vineyards and the sale of wines on the international market.

The ministry of Amos reflects this prosperity. He could see the great houses in Samaria where the rich lived and he could see the hovels that housed the poor. He could see elaborate furniture being manufactured for the rich households and at Bethel he listened to the bragging of worshippers about the size of their freewill offerings and their elaborate sacrificial gifts.

New Empires Emerging

In 745 BC, Tiglath-Pileser became king of Assyria, and he was ambitious of expanding his empire westward towards the Mediterranean Sea. He captured Damascus in 732 BC and occupied part of northern Israel. Ten years later his son carried out a full-scale invasion of Israel and laid siege to Samaria 722 – 721 BC. Assyria then began a prolonged policy of population transfer, taking whole communities from different townships and resettling them in different parts of its empire. The policy was clearly aimed at destroying nationalism and thereby minimising the threat of revolt against Assyrian rule. It created the Samaritan people.

The prophecies of Amos make no reference to the international situation and although there are powerful warnings of disaster, there is no mention of the source of the violence he prophesied. It was a time of prosperity for both Judah and Israel. The rich became more wealthy, and the poor increasingly oppressed. Slavery was common in Israel among the poor and the luxury among the rich led to widespread injustice and corruption at all levels of society. Bribery and corruption became commonplace which inevitably favoured the rich and powerful, while leaving the poor suffering from institutional injustice.

The description given by Amos of life in the marketplace is highly revealing. He had obviously spent some time observing the practices of the market traders and the way they cheated the poor. He had seen the dishonest scales used by the traders and how they mixed the sweepings in with the wheat. Worst of all, he saw the ruthlessness of the legal system in denying justice to the poor and reducing them to slavery.

A brief account of these events is given in 2 Kings 14:23-28, but the editors of Kings and Chronicles are not particularly friendly towards the northern kingdom of Israel so there is no celebration of Jeroboam's achievements. He built up a strong army with many chariots and he also fortified cities and especially strengthened the defences of Samaria. His supremacy over Syria was particularly significant because this provided a buffer for Israel and Judah against the rising power of Assyria, particularly after the advent of Tiglath-Pileser in 745 BC.

The death of Jeroboam II in 752 BC after a reign of 41 years was followed by a period of rapid instability and political struggle for the leadership of the nation. Jeroboam II was succeeded by his son Zechariah but only six months later he was assassinated by Shallum who also was murdered just one month later by Menahem. Menahem lasted for 10 years during which time he paid tribute to Assyria. In order to pay for this, he extorted money from wealthy families which led to considerable unrest in the nation.

Menahem was succeeded by his son Pekahiah who lasted two years before he was assassinated by Pekah who reigned for 20 years. During his reign Ahaz became king of Judah while Pekah made an agreement with Rezin, king of Syria, to form an alliance to defend their nations against the threat of invasion from Assyria. They tried to persuade Ahaz to join with them but to no avail, so Israel and Syria combined to invade Judah, laying siege to Jerusalem.

Ahaz responded by sending to Assyria asking for help and sending a gift of silver and gold. Assyria then attacked Damascus in 732 BC and deported its citizens to Assyria. This left Israel standing alone against Assyria. Tiglath-Pileser invaded Israel taking Gilead and the Galilee and deporting large numbers of the people to Assyria. This led to Hoshea conspiring against Pekah and assassinating him.

Hoshea became the last king of Israel, reigning for nine years. At first, he paid tribute to Assyria and made an agreement to be Shalmaneser's vassal, but he foolishly sent to Egypt for help. When

Shalmaneser discovered that Hoshea was a traitor, he invaded the entire territory of Israel, capturing and destroying Samaria, Bethel and other cities, continuing the policy of his predecessor and resettling people from other parts of Assyria into Israel. All this is described in 2 Kings 14 – 17 and is the background to the ministry, not only of Amos, but of all four of the eighth century prophets of Israel and Judah – Amos, Isaiah of Jerusalem, Hosea and Micah.

Structure and Content of the Book of Amos

Some biblical scholars believe that there were originally two books of Amos that have been put together, but there is very little evidence of this in the Hebrew text. The opening verse says that it was compiled two years before the earthquake, but this is not a great help because there are no records enabling us to date this earthquake. The statement at the beginning of Amos says that Uzziah was king of Judah and Jeroboam II was king of Israel. Uzziah died in 744 BC and Jeroboam II died in 746 BC, so this gives us a fairly accurate assessment that Amos' ministry was about the middle of the eighth century BC. As Amos does not mention any other king this may indicate that his ministry occupied quite a small timespan, quite unlike Isaiah's which stretched over most of the second half of the eighth century.

The book falls roughly into two parts, the first part dealing first with the sins of Israel's Gentile neighbours. This leads into a strong denunciation of Israel which is clearly the main focus of interest. It draws to a conclusion in chapter four with evidence of Israel's spiritual blindness in not rightly interpreting the signs of warning that God had given which varied from drought and plagues to military reverses.

The second part begins with a lament and the threat of judgement, warning that the 'day of the Lord' would not be a day of blessing but a day of judgement against Israel. This is followed by four pictures, or visions, that are interpreted as threats of judgement. The third and fourth are interrupted by an encounter with Amaziah the priest of Bethel who drove Amos out of the town.

The book ends with the direct prophecy of the destruction of the nation of Israel that they will be removed *"from the face of the earth"*, but there will be a remnant of survivors, and the final promise is for a time of restoration after a period of exile.

1 THE WORDS OF AMOS   Amos 1:1

The words of Amos, one of the shepherds of Tekoa – what he saw concerning Israel two years before the earthquake.

This introductory statement is quite important for understanding of the style and message of Amos. It tells us that Amos was a shepherd from Tekoa, some 10 miles south of Jerusalem. Tekoa was an important town fortified by Rehoboam the son of King Solomon who lacked his father's wisdom. He followed young men who gave him the wrong advice (2 Chron 10:8). This gave Jeroboam the opportunity for which he waited in exile from Solomon. He returned from Egypt in 922 BC and led a revolt of the 10 tribes of Israel, leaving only Judah and Benjamin in the south of the country.

Rehoboam did not go to war against Jeroboam; instead, he fortified some fifteen towns from Bethlehem in the south of Judah to Hebron in the north, including major cities such as Azekah. He strengthened their defences and put commanders in charge of each so they could resist attack from Jeroboam. He also distributed his own sons around the fortified cities of Judah to ensure that his dynasty survived any attack from the northern kingdom of Israel.

The split between North and South was completed by Jeroboam rejecting the priests and Levites who served the God of Israel and, *"He appointed his own priests for the high places and for the goat and calf idols he had made"* (2 Chron 11:15). Jeroboam appointed priests from among the ordinary people. A man could pay for his priesthood with *"a young bull and seven rams"* and then he became consecrated (2 Chron 13:9).

The Levites who had land in the northern kingdom, left their homes and moved into Judah, refusing to serve the golden calf idols set up by Jeroboam at places like Bethel and Gilgal. The priests and Levites all concentrated their services upon the temple in Jerusalem. During the lifetime of Rehoboam, although the tensions between North and South continued, there was no open warfare. This was largely due to the intervention of the Prophet Shemaiah who said, *"Do not go out to fight against your brothers. Go home, every one of you"* (2 Chron 11:4).

Nevertheless, the Egyptians invaded Judah and stripped Jerusalem of much of the wealth left by Solomon. Rehoboam reigned for 17 years, he was followed by his son Abijah during whose reign there was a major battle between Israel and Judah that ended in Jeroboam being routed and Judah triumphing. Jeroboam actually reigned some 40 years and stabilised the nation with many people moving from the countryside into the towns and cities where trade was flourishing and the pursuit of wealth became dominant. The predominant mood in the nation by the time of Jeroboam II some 150 years later was the enjoyment of prosperity and a culture of complacency.

It was against this historical background that Amos began his ministry as a Southerner in the North. The date of his ministry was said to be 'two years before the earthquake' during the reign of Uzziah king of Judah which was 768 – 740 BC. The reign of Jeroboam II was 793 – 752. It is not possible to determine the years of Amos' ministry precisely, but most biblical scholars agree that his activity would have been somewhere between 760 and 750 BC. This was just slightly before the rise of Tiglath-Pileser as king of Assyria and the beginning of the expansion of his empire, capturing Damascus in 732 and destroying Samaria 10 years later in 722-1 BC.

Amos is said to be a 'seeing prophet', the words are *"what he saw concerning Israel"*, which means that he was a visionary who received words of inspiration through visual images. This is not unusual: Jeremiah often saw pictures through which he received a word from the Lord. The very first word he received was through looking at the branch of an almond tree (Jer 1:11).

We know very little about Amos, but he himself told the priest of Bethel "*I was neither a prophet nor a prophet's son, but I was a shepherd, and I also took care of sycamore trees*" (7:14). As noted in the Introduction the Hebrew word here for 'shepherd' is also, in 2 Kings 3:4 where the king of Mesha is said to be a shepherd. Amos clearly was no ordinary shepherd, so he may have been a land-owning farmer of substance. But really, we know no details of his life and nothing of his family background. He is, nevertheless, recognised as a man of great insight and courage, blowing the opening trumpet of warning of immense significance that sets the tone for the three men of God who followed him.

2 THE LORD ROARS   Amos 1:2

The Lord roars from Zion and thunders from Jerusalem, the pastures of the shepherds dry up, and the top of Carmel withers.

The words of Amos begin with a small piece of poetry. Hebrew poetry does not usually rhyme but there is a definite rhyme in this little piece. There is also a parallelism that is much more characteristic of Hebrew poetry. 'Roars' and 'thunders' are parallel; and 'dry up' and 'withers' are another parallel. The purpose of this little piece of poetry is unclear. It is said to be words from the Lord coming from Jerusalem which would certainly not endear Amos to the people of Samaria or Bethel in the northern kingdom of Israel where Amos was sent to minister. Most biblical scholars conclude that this is an editorial addition added later when the words of Amos were brought to Jerusalem after the destruction of Samaria in 722 BC. But this misses an important point that Amos himself was from Judah and he would no doubt have believed that the word of the Lord would go out from Jerusalem.

The Lord roaring from Jerusalem is important for the message it conveys. It summarises the whole purpose of the book of Amos which is a declaration of the judgement of God upon sin and that the time of judgement had now come. Its primary direction was towards the northern kingdom of Israel, but it was also directed towards Judah, despite beginning with words directed at the neighbouring nations. The urgent message here is directed towards Israel 30 years before the destruction of Samaria by the Assyrians.

The warning was that the whole countryside would be 'dried up', from the low grasslands of the shepherds in the valleys to the top of Mount Carmel. This was carried out by the scorched earth policy of destructive cruelty pursued with indiscriminate slaughter by the Assyrians. This was the last warning that Israel would be given. Amos noted a sign to confirm the message of the word of the Lord: drought was currently affecting the whole land from the pastures in the valleys, to the tops of Carmel.

The major significance of this declaration that the 'Lord roars from Zion' is missed by most commentators and it was certainly misunderstood by the people of Israel. It was thought that God, who had so often roared against the enemies of Israel was now roaring against his own people in judgement. Certainly, this is how it was interpreted later on when, first the northern kingdom of Israel was utterly destroyed, and then Judah was overwhelmed and Jerusalem was burnt down and the temple destroyed by the Babylonians in 586 BC. A Psalm of lament that comes from that time accuses God of breaking his covenant vows, *"You have renounced the covenant with your servant and have defiled his crown in the dust"* (Ps 89:39); although God had promised *"nor will I ever betray my faithfulness. I will not violate my covenant"* (Ps 89:33-34).

The truth that is overlooked is that there are two very different kinds of roaring of lions. The male lion's roar announces his intention of springing upon his prey, whereas the female lion who has small cubs in her care has quite a different intention in her roar. She warns of danger, but her roar is a call to her cubs to come to her. The moment they hear that tremendous roar the cubs come running to her and take shelter under her caring protection.

This is the purpose of the roar in the opening statement of Amos. It is warning the people that the time of peace and prosperity enjoyed for more than a century since the time of King David had come to an end and there were enemies on the horizon threatening terrible destruction. The roar is also a call from God to his people to come running to him, for only in him is there any safety. The message was that the people had departed from the way of the Lord – indulging in idolatry through the Canaanite shrines in direct contravention of the covenant. They were further breaking the covenant by turning away from the Torah into sinful ways of injustice, bribery and corruption, oppressing the poor and ignoring the teaching of Moses. All this would lead inevitably to a time of judgement that would befall them unless they repent and turn, running to God.

If they did repent and turn to the Lord they would immediately be forgiven and restored into fellowship with God which would also bring them under his protection. If they returned to him, the roar of God from Zion would be the roar of a male lion against the enemies of Israel which would guarantee the protection of the people of Israel and of Judah.

3 JUDGEMENT UPON DAMASCUS   Amos 1:3-5

For three sins of Damascus, even for four, I will not turn back my wrath.

In verses 3 to 5 we have the first of the series of seven judgement passages directed at the neighbouring nations around Israel. They each begin with the same formula, recounting three or four sins which have incurred the wrath of Yahweh. Only one or two sins are described in detail in each of the seven nations that are covered in chapters 1 and 2. When we reach chapter 2:6f where attention is turned upon Israel (which is the whole purpose of the piece), the details become much more explicit. This was the reason why Amos as a Southerner from Judah had been sent to the northern kingdom of Israel. His mission was to take a strong word of warning of the terrible destruction that he had seen revealed to him.

Amos makes no mention of Assyria and he does not describe the developing international scene which presents a threat to the small independent nations around Israel. His task is not political but it is purely a spiritual mission dealing with the sins of the nation that had put them on a path that was destined to bring disaster upon the nation. He knew that only God could save them from the coming international storm because their sins had broken the covenant and thereby put them outside the protection of God.

In the passage we are considering today, the focus is upon Syria, *"For three sins of Damascus, even for four, I will not turn back my wrath."* It is interesting that only the name of 'Damascus' is included here when the subject is the whole nation of Syria. Damascus is the oldest city in the world with parts that can be traced back 2000 years. There had been hostility between Israel and the kings of Damascus ever since the settlement in Canaan. Three or four sins are listed but only one is detailed. The word 'sin', translated as 'trespass' in the King James Version, is *peshe* in the Hebrew which comes from the root *pesha* meaning 'to fall away' or to 'turn away' from something. In this case it means that Damascus had turned away from the basic standards of righteousness required by God, such as those set out in the Decalogue.

We cannot be certain of when this particular incident occurred that is referred to here. There were numerous incidents of conflict between Israel and Syria such as those referred to in 2 Kings 8 where Elisha went to Damascus and told Hazael that he would become king of Syria. Elisha wept because he foresaw some of the wicked cruelty that Damascus would inflict upon the people of Israel (2 Kings 8:12).

This is the most heinous cruelty that could be inflicted by human beings on another nation. The sin selected is not detailed anywhere else in the Bible. There is, however, a reference in 2 Kings 10:32 to an incident during the reign of King Jehu that had occurred earlier which involved Hazael and Benhadad, kings of Syria. It was during a time of war, when Israel lost a lot of territory to Syria that included most of the land east of the Jordan, *"The region of Gad, Reuben and Manasseh, from Aoer by the Arnon Gorge through Gilead to Bashan."*

Amos says that God would *"not turn back his wrath",* which is difficult in the Hebrew which literally says, *"I will not cause it to return."* This means that God would not change his mind. Probably the NEB is right saying, *"I shall grant them no reprieve. Because she threshed Gilead with sledges having iron teeth."*

It was a farming practice to use heavy planks of wood with iron nails driven through them that are dragged through a cornfield, threshing the corn by separating the wheat from the chaff. Syria won an overwhelming victory leaving the entire army of Israel either dead or badly wounded on the battlefield. Then they committed the heinous crime of threshing the battlefield with iron sledges pulled over the wounded as well as the dead, scattering body parts everywhere.

Judgement by fire was threatened and Damascus would be under siege. The great wooden bar that was used to secure the gates when they were shut would be broken and the gate would be flung open to the enemy. Judgement would fall upon the king of Syria because of the sins of Damascus and the people of the land would go into exile.

In the final statement Yahweh would destroy the king of Syria in the valley of Aven, or the Valley of Wickedness, and the people taken to Kir – an unknown location. About 30 years after this prophecy the Assyrians swept through Syria. They destroyed Damascus in 732 BC and took many of the inhabitants to other parts of their Empire. Thus, the prophecy was fulfilled.

4 JUDGEMENT ON THE PHILISTINES   Amos 1:6-10

This is what the Lord says: "For three sins of Gaza, even for four, I will not turn back my wrath because she took captive whole communities and sold them to Edom."

The Philistines were implacable enemies of Israel from the earliest days of recorded history. Shortly after the children of Israel had escaped from Egypt, Moses requested permission to pass through territory held by Gaza and this was refused. The Philistines caused a lot of problems in the time of Saul and David. They were eventually subdued during David's reign and Solomon then established his empire over the whole region and Gaza became just another area within the land of Israel. After the division of the land into Israel in the North and Judah in the south, the five cities of Gaza became part of Judah.

Amos says that Gaza *"took captive whole communities and sold them to Edom"* which is the crime for which judgement was going to fall upon Gaza. The kings of Ashdod, Ashkelon and Ekron and their cities would be destroyed *"until the last of the Philistines is dead"*.

This presents us with a number of difficulties. Clearly prophecy that all Philistines would be killed has never been fulfilled. Their descendants, the Palestinians, the people of Gaza are there today, still presenting problems for the people of Israel.

Historically there is no record in the history of Israel that we can clearly identify with the charge that Philistines took whole communities and sold them to Edom. There is, however, an account in 2 Chronicles 21 that may be the incident to which Amos is referring. It follows the only writing we have from the hand of the Prophet Elijah in 2 Chron 21:12-15, which sets out the sins of Jehoram, son of Jehoshaphat who, on inheriting the throne had murdered all his brothers and set up high places for worship across the countryside.

Elijah's letter was followed by the statement, *"The Lord aroused against Jehoram the hostility of the Philistines and of the Arabs who lived near the Cushites"* (2 Chron 21:16). They invaded Judah and sacked Jerusalem, carrying away *"all the goods found in the king's palace, together with his sons and wives. Not a son was left to him except Ahaziah, the youngest."* The *"whole community"* taken by the Philistines and sold to Edom as slaves may have been most of the population of Jerusalem. This could have been the heinous sin that Amos identified because Edom were renowned for their cruelty and their hatred of the people of Israel.

A similar charge of taking whole communities of captive people from Israel and selling them to the people of Edom is the major charge against the people of Tyre. This was disregarding a treaty of brotherhood that had been established during the reign of Solomon. The whole of 1 Kings 5 is devoted to the treaty established between Hiram king of Tyre and Solomon by which Hiram kept Solomon supplied with all the cedar and pine logs needed for the building of the temple. This treaty was building upon a friendship established between the king of Tyre and King David.

Solomon recruited large numbers of men and sent them to Lebanon to assist in the work of cutting timber for the temple. Solomon also gave to King Hiram large quantities of food for his household that included wheat and olive oil. This arrangement was sealed in the statement, *"There were peaceful relations between Hiram and Solomon, and the two of them made a treaty"* (1 Kgs 5:12).

Everything went wrong in the relationship between the peoples of Israel and Tyre when King Ahab married the Princess Jezebel of Tyre which was probably to cement a treaty of friendship between the two nations. Jezebel brought with her a large number of priests to Samaria. This was strongly opposed by Elijah, climaxing in the confrontation on Mount Carmel when Elijah and his followers slaughtered 450 of the prophets of Baal in the Kishon Valley (1 Kgs 18:40).

The killing of these men was regarded as a direct insult to the people of Tyre resulting in deep hostility.

Tyre was well known for dealing in slavery since the rise of the Phoenicians and their trading empire stretching across the shores of the Mediterranean. But why the rulers of Edom would be interested in purchasing whole communities of Israelites from Tyre as well as from the Philistines is a mystery. The answer may be in Ezekiel 27:13 referring to the gross sin of slavery from which Tyre made immense wealth. Amos pronounced the judgement of God upon the injustice and cruelty of trading in human beings, incurring the wrath of God that would bring fire upon the walls of Tyre. Indeed, it did!

5 JUDGEMENT UPON EDOM AND AMMON
Amos 1:11-15

For three sins of Edom, even for four, I will not turn back my wrath. Because he pursued his brother with the sword, stifling all compassion.

The relationship between Edom and Israel goes right back to Jacob and Esau and the conflict between the brothers who were constantly against each other. Their rivalry began in the womb when the boys were said to have been jostling with each other. Rebecca, in her prayer was told, *"Two nations are in your womb, and two peoples from within you will be separated . . . And the older will serve the younger"* (Gen 25:23).

Esau was the older brother who was born first and therefore should have been the one to inherit his father's blessing. But this was usurped by Jacob by deception that made a lasting impression upon the relationship between the brothers. There was conflict between the two brothers right from childhood. Esau became a skilful hunter while Jacob preferred staying quietly among the community. The account of how Esau sold his birthright for some food was a story that would have been very well known in the eighth century BC when Amos began his ministry. The hostility between Jacob and Esau would have been part of the folk history that was passed down the centuries (Gen 25:34).

Esau's descendants settled in the land just south of that occupied by Israel known as *"the hill country of Seir"* (Gen 36:8). There was constant tension between the two peoples and both David and Solomon ruled Edom, but it gained its independence during the time of Rehoboam. Elath was an important centre in Edom that changed hands several times. Azariah took it for Judah (2 Kgs 14:22), but it was retaken for Edom by Rezin king of Syria about the year 735 BC (2 Kgs 16:6). This was actually after the time of Amos, but he was reflecting the hostility between the two brothers over many centuries and the ruthless cruelty shown by the people of Edom which Amos says would bring them under the judgement of God.

The hostility and cruelty of Edom reached a new height in 586 BC when the Babylonians sacked Jerusalem. The Edomites poured over the borders into Judah, rejoicing at the downfall of the people of Israel. They not only participated in looting Jerusalem but actually established settlements in the land which caused enormous anger among the exiles in Babylon. This is reflected in a prophecy by Ezekiel 25:12-14. The judgement foreseen by Amos certainly was fulfilled when the Babylonians attacked shortly after the fall of Jerusalem.

Like the people of Edom, the Ammonites were also charged with cruelty. Their crimes were not the usual cruelty in battle exercised by one army upon another. Amos charged them with crimes against humanity – deliberately targeting civilians in a time of war. They carried out the most monstrous crimes of ripping open pregnant women at Gilead in what Amos described as a border war. This was a particularly cruel practice that was outlawed by most nations and would be what undoubtedly today would be classified as a 'war crime'.

Amos declared that God's punishment would be severe and that the walls of Rabbah – modern day Amman – would be destroyed by fire. The people of Ammon would be subjected to particularly violent warfare and that her kings would go into exile together with all the leading officials. This was a prophecy that was fulfilled soon after the fall of Jerusalem in 586 when the Babylonians swept through Ammon and destroyed Rabbah and most of the towns and villages of Ammon. They left the land in such a state of devastation that it lasted for the next 400 years when there was no national government. The land was occupied by wandering tribes of Arabs who ate most the vegetation leaving the land largely barren.

It is interesting to note that Amos' description of the fire that would destroy Rabbah as part of the wrath of God being poured out upon the nation used the same words in Hebrew found in Psalm 83 which is the Psalm most quoted in relation to the hatred of Israel by Gentile nations. *"Come, they say, let us destroy them as a nation, that the name of Israel be remembered no more"* (Ps 83:4). The similarity between Amos 1:14 and Psalm 83:15 is there with the same words signifying violent storm with winds that drive the fires of judgement upon the walls of Rabbah.

Psalm 83 is very relevant for all the neighbouring nations around Israel that are dealt with in the first two chapters of Amos. He sees the common denominator as the hatred of the Lord's people of Israel which results in acts of cruelty that incur the wrath of God upon them.

6 JUDGEMENT UPON MOAB AND JUDAH
Amos 2:1-5

This is what the Lord says: "For three sins of Moab, even for four, I will not turn back my wrath. Because he burned as if to lime, the bones of Edom's king."

The first relationship between Israel and Moab is recorded in Numbers 25:1-3 when the people of Israel under the leadership of Moses were staying at Shittim on their journey towards Canaan. *"The men began to indulge in sexual immorality with the Moabite women, who invited them to the sacrifices to their gods."* This led to the deaths of 24,000 people in a plague.

The land occupied by Moab was south of Ammon and east of the Dead Sea. Relationships between Moab and Israel were rarely friendly even though we know that people from Israel during a time of famine were welcomed in Moab where Elimelech and Naomi went, and their two boys married Moabite girls one of whom was Ruth, who returned to Bethlehem with her widowed mother-in-law after the death of Elimelech and both of his sons.

Ruth was the grandmother of David who became king of Israel, but this did not make David any more friendly towards Moab. In 2 Samuel 8:2 there is a record of David defeating Moab and killing a large number of men, but in 2 Kings 3:5 it says, *"The king of Moab rebelled against the king of Israel. So at that time King Joram set out from Samaria and mobilised all Israel."* He invited Judah and Edom to join the mission to subdue Moab. Jehoshaphat agreed and after some long marches they slaughtered the Moabites and destroyed towns. *"When the king of Moab saw that the battle had gone against him, he took his firstborn son . . . and offered him as a sacrifice on the city wall"* (2 Kgs 3:26-27). This so horrified everyone that the armies of Judah and Israel returned home.

The whole incident had generated extreme hatred for Edom in Moab. Hence the crime for which Amos charges Moab is not for any sin against Israel but against Edom. Moab had taken the bones of Edom's king and burnt them to lime. Most biblical scholars interpret this as having taken place at Petra where bones were placed in caves that were considered sacrosanct. The Moabites cared for none of these things, and they burnt the remains of Edom's king which was an act of desecration. Amos says that Moab will be judged by fire amidst great tumults and the blast of trumpets. It was traditional to accompany the sacrifice of children by great drum rolls and blasts of trumpets, no doubt to drown the cries of the children.

Judgement upon Judah

It is interesting to note that the only charge that Amos brings against his home nation of Judah is not about any acts of war or physical crimes. It is entirely spiritual. They had rejected the Torah given to them by the Lord and not kept his decrees. Instead, they had been led astray into idolatry, following the gods of their ancestors.

Amos sounds very much like the other writing prophets. He is fully in line with the charges that Isaiah of Jerusalem had given before him, and 150 years later others like Jeremiah and Ezekiel would also declare in similar words. At the time of Amos' ministry Uzziah was king of Judah. He had developed a powerful army and had carried out a successful campaign against the Philistines (2 Chron 26:6). It is recorded that, *"After Uzziah became powerful, pride led to his downfall. He was unfaithful to the Lord his God and entered the temple of the Lord to burn incense on the altar of incense"* (2 Chron 26:16).

It was at this point that leprosy was noted on Uzziah's face and he was banned from the temple and from public life. His son Jothan acted as regent until his death. If we are right in the timing and this became known in Samaria, it would certainly have been seen as an outcome of the condemnation declared by Amos. His declaration that the people of Judah had been led astray by false gods was certainly true of the whole history of Israel.

From the time of Moses, there had been idolatry among the people. The central problem was rejecting the Torah, ignoring the teaching of the Lord. This had been the sin of the people of Israel ever since they left the 'Great Assembly' at Mount Sinai where they had worshipped the golden calf. A few years before Amos, Isaiah had declared, *"They have rejected the law of the Lord Almighty and spurned the word of the Holy One of Israel. Therefore, the Lord's anger burns against his people"* (Is 5:24-25).

7 JUDGEMENT ON ISRAEL   Amos 2:6-16

This is what the Lord says: "For three sins of Israel, even for four, I will not turn back my wrath. They sell the righteous for silver, and the needy for a pair of sandals."

Amos had now reached the point that was the original purpose of his mission – to declare the word of God to the people of the kingdom of Israel. All these pronouncements would have been given in public either in Samaria or at Bethel. We cannot be certain of the location, but he would undoubtedly have had a crowd who would have been delighted to hear the condemnation of neighbouring nations. There would no doubt have be great cheering when Amos declared the word of the Lord against Damascus, Gaza, Tyre, Edom, Ammon and Moab.

When Amos as a Southerner, which would have been obvious from his accent, spoke about the sins of Judah, the crowd would have been even more delighted. Then he turned his attention upon Israel and no doubt the crowd would have become silent or restive, or some may even have made hostile comments. Amos persisted – the unrighteousness of the leaders of this affluent nation basking in complacency was almost indescribable, but he had been sent by God to declare the word of the Lord in judgement upon slavery practised by the rich and the injustice and oppression of the poor and powerless.

Maybe, by this point, many in the crowd were those who suffered from the evil practices of the rich and powerful politicians. They would have begun to warm to the fearlessness of this stranger from the south who had bravely come among them. He said publicly that he was not from a prophetic background – there were no prophets in his family – he was just an ordinary man whom God had chosen for a mission to his people, but the message he was declaring was indeed the word of God!

Amos persisted: not only did the rich and powerful people trample on the heads of the poor, denying them justice but they were utterly depraved in their personal morality, father and son using the same girl for their sexual appetites. They even trampled on the poor by taking garments given in pledge and not returning them at night for the poor man to wrap around his body in the cold night air! The rich had no standards of morality, they only cared for themselves! These words would have gone down very well with many people in the crowd who knew that they were true and would have been delighted to hear them as a word from God.

Amos, by this time, was fully into his stride and he began drawing upon the history of Israel, declaring God saying, *"I destroyed the Amorite before them though he was tall as the cedars and strong as the oaks. I destroyed his fruit above and his roots below."* This reference to the settlement in Canaan looked back to the time when the people of Israel were brought out of Egypt and led through the desert. Throughout their history God had raised up prophets among them. This is the theme that Jeremiah picked up more than a century later: *"From the time your forefathers left Egypt until now, day after day, again and again I sent you my servants the prophets. But they did not listen to me or pay attention"* (Jer 7:25-26).

It is very possible that Jeremiah had read the words of Amos, and he was happy to declare similar words in Jerusalem which would have been as unpopular among the people in Jerusalem as they were hated by the people of Samaria. Amos persisted, saying that God had raised up Nazirites from among the young men of Israel, but Israel had forced the Nazirites to drink wine and reject the prophets that God had raised among them. This was the height of wickedness and God was going to bring swift judgement upon the people of Israel.

The Nazirites did not cut their hair or drink wine. Their origins went back to Joseph who was said to be a 'Prince among his brothers'. The Hebrew verb *'nazar'* from which we get the noun *'nazir'* is used here. Nazir is *'a separated one'* – separated for a purpose – from his brothers and from the rest of the community. The traditions go back to Numbers 6 where Moses spoke of their separation unto the Lord.

Amos used this outrage against the Nazirites as his final illustration of the sins of the people that would bring upon their heads the judgement of God. This would be swift and powerful. It would overcome the much-vaunted army of Israel, and both foot soldiers and horsemen would flee for their lives on the day of God's judgement.

8 ISRAEL JUDGEMENT ON THE CHOSEN ONES
Amos 3:1-8

Hear this word the Lord has spoken against you, O people of Israel- against the whole family I brought up out of Egypt. "You only have I chosen of all the families of the earth."

All the writing prophets had a companion who wrote down their words and this opening statement is most likely to have been an editorial introduction to the words of Amos. Most biblical scholars agree that the words of Amos could not have remained in Samaria after its destruction in 722 BC by the Assyrians. His words would have been taken to Jerusalem where scribes would have seen their relevance to Judah. Hence the words *"the whole family I brought up out of Egypt"* were included.

The opening words of Amos, *"You only have I chosen of all the families of the earth,"* would have immediately spoken a word of comfort to his hearers in Israel. God had not rejected them despite the sins of Jeroboam and the breakaway from Judah and the erection of a golden calf at Bethel! But in fact, the words *"you only have I chosen"* were not a message of comfort but were leading to a devastating pronouncement of judgement upon their sin of not recognising the responsibility that went with the great privilege of being chosen by God. Moses had warned the people at Mount Sinai that they were only chosen because God wanted to use them – the family of Abraham – to reveal himself to the world. Therefore, they had to be different, separated from all other nations.

Amos followed this with a series of rhetorical questions each of which demanded the answer 'no'. The questions were not delivered as a word from God, but as questions from the prophet, designed to show cause and effect, event and outcome. All seven events led up to the pronouncement in verse 7, *"Surely the Sovereign Lord does nothing without revealing his plan to his servants the prophets."*

The blunt statement of judgement with which Amos began would no doubt have raised questions among his hearers regarding his own authority. Who was this stranger from Judah? What gave him the right to pronounce judgement on us? Hence, each of the seven rhetorical questions is designed to establish the authority of Amos. Many different explanations have been offered by theologians for the meaning of "*Do two walk together unless they have agreed to do so?*" The most likely view is that the two are Israel and God. Unless Israel is walking in God's way there can be no agreement, and this is why Amos has been sent with this message of warning. There is real danger facing the nation the same way as the roar of the lion indicates that there is real danger because he is about to pounce. In the same way, the bird only falls into the trap when it is loaded, and the trumpet is only sounded in the city when there is danger facing the citizens.

Amos is establishing his authority. He is not there simply to pronounce his own ideas, but he is a messenger from God in the same way as Moses was sent to Egypt with a message from God, and others have been called as prophets with a message to the nation throughout the history of Israel. It is God who gives a message to the prophet, and it is given by revelation. The prophet is the servant of God who reveals something to the prophet that is hidden from the world.

The Hebrew word used here is *gala* which literally means 'uncovering a secret'. Amos is saying that something of great importance that is hidden from the leaders of Israel has been revealed to him and this is why he has come all the way from Judah to declare this warning. When the Sovereign Lord speaks to the prophet, he cannot keep quiet – he has to deliver the message in the same way as someone who hears the roar of a lion has to take heed of the warning.

Jeremiah faced the same responsibility. For 40 years Jeremiah walked the streets of Jerusalem telling everyone who would listen to him that there was great danger facing the nation, but no one would heed his warning. He says, *"But if I say, I will not mention him or speak any more name, his word is in my heart like a fire, a fire shut up in my bones. I am weary of holding it in, indeed, I cannot"* (Jer 20:9). This word clearly summarises the mission of the prophet who receives a revelation from God which he is compelled to deliver. *"The Sovereign Lord has spoken – who can but prophesy?"* This was why Amos had come to Samaria. He was a man with a message and a mission to deliver it.

9 THE MESSAGE OF WARNING   Amos 3:9-15

Proclaim to the fortresses of Ashdod and to the fortresses of Egypt: "Assemble yourselves on the mountains of Samaria."

Amos had begun his message to Israel with a powerful warning in 3:2, *"You only have I chosen . . . Therefore, I will punish you for all your sins."* In these verses he returns to that statement and calls upon the whole world to come and witness what was going on in Israel. He selects a city in Gaza that is unknown, but most biblical scholars think that Amos was simply selecting Egypt and the Philistines as representative of all those who are the enemies of Israel.

Amos is so strongly motivated to bring this warning to Israel, the chosen people of God, that he selects representatives of the world who all present a threat to Israel, to come and see what is going on in Samaria that will cause God to remove his cover of protection over the land and bring judgement upon them for their sins. This extreme of punishment will be part of God's purpose in revealing his nature and purposes to the world. But in summoning the Gentiles to come as witnesses – that should act as the strongest possible warning to God's chosen people. It should say to them that even the ungodly nations of the world would be shocked at what was going on in Israel!

In order to understand the message of these verses it is essential to see them in the context of the situation during the reign of Jeroboam II. It was an age of peace and prosperity. A number of the cities of Israel had been fortified and Jeroboam had built up a powerful army that he boasted would deter any enemy of Israel from invasion. He extended the borders of Israel, capturing Damascus and Syria. It gave a sense of stability and safety to the people, and this encouraged productivity and trade. The values of the nation were centred upon the accumulation of wealth.

A lot of families moved in from the countryside to the towns and enjoyed the prosperity generated through the lines of international trade that developed. This produced a generation of rich merchants and a general atmosphere of complacency seen in the elaborate furniture and lifestyles of the rich which contrasted strongly with the poor who were suffering from injustice and oppression. This was a major part of the message that Amos brought: *"They do not know how to do right, declares the Lord, who hoard plunder and loot in their fortresses."* Their homes, with all the facilities that money could buy, were their fortresses – their citadels of luxury demonstrating their wealth.

"They do not know how to do right" is an important statement. The Hebrew word used is *nachoach* which literally means *'straight'* – the people did not know how to go straight, because their values were crooked, corrupted by neglecting the word of the Lord so they had not followed a straight path. There was injustice, oppression, and violence among the people in the pursuit of wealth.

The death of Jeroboam II was followed by a series of kings who were assassinated, recorded in 2 Kings 15, which created a time of great instability that encouraged the Assyrians to attack Israel and demand tribute. An agreement was made but when Hoshea became king he entered into a secret agreement with Egypt which led to full-scale invasion by Assyria and a three-year siege of Samaria. The Assyrians then deported 27,000 people from Israel, resettling them in different parts of the Assyrian Empire. They also brought into the land people from many other parts of their Empire to occupy the towns and cities of Israel (2 Kings 17:24). As noted in the Introduction this created the Samaritans who were living in the northern part of Israel at the time of Jesus.

All this occurred about 40 years after the ministry of Amos and was clearly a catastrophe which was foreseen in the warning that he gave. That warning was vividly portrayed in 3:12, *"As a shepherd saves from the lion's mouth only two leg bones or a piece of an ear so will the Israelites be saved."* This was what was going to happen to the people of Samaria who would be scattered across the Assyrian Empire and lose their identity as the chosen people of God.

The disaster that would befall the people of Israel would include the destruction of the sanctuary they had constructed at Bethel with a golden calf at the centre of their worship. Amos says that *"On the day that I punish Israel for her sins, I will destroy the altars of Bethel."* All the elaborate houses of the rich would be destroyed, and their mansions demolished. All this was because they had departed from the ways of the Lord.

10 WARNING TO THE WOMEN   Amos 4:1-3

Hear this word, you cows of Bashan on Mount Samaria, you women who oppress the poor and crush the needy.

Amos certainly does not mince his words, and he is very much in line with the other writing prophets who often used colourful language in delivering their message. We should, however, beware of reading into this statement the pejorative strength that the words convey in our English translations today. The cattle on the verdant pastures of Bashan were renowned for their milk production. They were pictured as large fat beasts lazily strolling around their lush fields, eating and drinking all they needed.

The women of Samaria did no work and were pictured as overweight and over pampered. They lived lazy lives enjoying rich food and drink in total contrast to the poor who were oppressed and needy. The rich women in their elaborately furnished great houses were waited upon by their poor servants.

The charge that they were oppressing the poor and crushing the needy does not mean to say that they were directly involved in the oppression of the powerless, but they were certainly the beneficiaries of the power exercised by the men in the nation whose primary objective was the accumulation of wealth. They would stop at nothing in order to obtain their objectives, which is what Amos was referring to in saying, *"They sell the righteous for silver and the needy for a pair of sandals . . . and deny justice to the oppressed"* (2:6).

In any dispute the poor could get no justice because the legal system was rigged in favour of the rich who held all the power. The women undoubtedly benefited from this system which is what Amos is referring to here, but the statement that they say to their husbands *"bring us some drinks!"* is misleading. The word 'husbands' is certainly not in the Hebrew, although it appears in a number of different translations. The King James version (KJV) is probably nearer to the truth with, *"which say to their masters, 'Bring, and let us drink'."* It may be that Amos was simply referring to the fact that the rich women were waited upon by men in their households. It does not mean that women held all the power in the nation!

Amos continues to describe the threat that he sees for the future of Samaria, currently basking in its false sense of security and prosperity. The rich women were a token of all that was wrong in the nation, lounging in their little cities of wealth and luxury. They were totally unaware of the frailty of the security upon which their lifestyle was based. Amos had obviously been given a revelation of what was going to happen in the near future although he does not anywhere speak of the international scene or speak of the Assyrian Empire expanding. He simply describes the revelations he has been given of the unspeakable horror that will descend upon the people of Samaria. He says the time will come when the women who now lounge about in their little citadels of security will be dragged from their houses with hooks, no doubt kicking and screaming.

Amos foresees the walls of Samaria, of which all its citizens were so proud and which their foot soldiers and chariots were there to guard, come crashing down like the walls of Jericho. The statement that each of the women would go out straight through breaks in the wall is a deliberate reminder of Jericho where the army of Israel went straight in the breaks in the wall as they opened up. The hooks were like the hooks placed in the noses of the cattle as they were led out for slaughter on the way to the market.

The women would be powerless to resist the enemy when the walls came down and they were cast out from the city like the refuse that was thrown out for destruction. The word in most of our Bibles *"you will be cast out towards Harmon, declares the Lord,"* is a statement that nobody can understand. The word 'Harmon' is unique. It only comes here and nowhere else in the Bible, so we have no means of comparing it with its use elsewhere.

This statement would have come as an enormous shock to the people of Samaria listening to Amos. In the same way as the warnings given by other prophets were dismissed, so the people of Israel ignored the warnings they were given. They were so blind to the truth that they could not recognise a genuine word of God – the God who had taken the people of Israel for his own beloved ones – and who was now warning them of danger. This was the tragedy that would unfold just 30 years from the time that Amos declared them.

11 SACRIFICES AND FREEWILL OFFERINGS
Amos 4:4-5

Go to Bethel and sin, go to Gilgal and sin yet more. Bring your sacrifices every morning, your tithes every three years.

The NIV that we are using in this study says, *"Go to Bethel . . ."* The King James and most other Bible translations read, *"Come to Bethel . . ."* which is a better translation and indicates that Amos had moved from Samaria where he had delivered his devastating warning to the women and was now at what was known as the *'king's sanctuary'* (7:13).

It certainly gives more understanding to this piece if Amos was actually there in Bethel witnessing the people coming in large numbers to make their sacrifices at a festival. Bethel was a special place in the history of Israel where Abraham received the promise from God that the land of Canaan would be given to him and his descendants. He built an altar there (Gen 12:8). It was also the place where Jacob had his famous dream and he renamed the place 'Bethel', 'House of God' – originally Luz (Gen 28:19).

Amos named both Bethel and Gilgal as places where the people of Israel were going to sin, or as the King James version and others render, 'trespass'. This is a better translation than 'sin', because the Hebrew word here is *pasha* which literally means 'to break a covenant'. The same word is found in 2 Kings 1:1 where it means 'rebellion'. Amos was saying here that by coming to Bethel the people of Israel were actually breaking the covenant with the Lord.

Most biblical scholars believe that Amos said this because he was from Judah where everyone believed that Jerusalem was the only place for worshipping God. Amos said that going to Gilgal was also 'trespassing' against God. Gilgal was the place where the people of Israel first stopped on entering the Promised Land and it was one of the two places where Jeroboam I had established a place of worship for the people of Israel when the 10 tribes broke from Rehoboam. This was considered a great sin of rebellion by the writers of Kings and Chronicles.

Nevertheless, Jeroboam, in Kings 11:26f, is shown as a good man who did not like what Solomon was doing in taking wives from pagan countries and building sanctuaries for them in Israel. A prophet named Ahijah prophesied over Jeroboam saying that God had chosen him to lead the 10 tribes of Israel, and that God was promising, *"I will build for you a dynasty as enduring as the one I built for David and will give Israel to you"* (1 Kgs 11:38).

This goes against the history of Israel as recorded in Kings and Chronicles from this time onwards where the scribes in Jerusalem regarded Jeroboam's action in 922 BC as a great sin. The kingdom of Israel lasted exactly 200 years until Samaria was destroyed by the Assyrians in 722 BC. The Assyrians had then attacked Jerusalem, but God heeded the prayers of Hezekiah and Isaiah and struck the Assyrians by plague forcing their withdrawal.

The history of the two kingdoms existing side-by-side was all written and edited by scribes in Jerusalem who clearly regarded everything in the northern kingdom as being in rebellion against God. Most biblical commentaries take the view that Amos was reflecting this same prejudice against the kingdom of Israel and that his words about worshipping at Bethel and Gilgal were sarcastic – that he was saying that in going to these places that Jeroboam had set up, so that the people in the 10 tribes of Israel did not have to go to Jerusalem, was sinful.

An alternative view that makes a lot more sense is that what Amos was doing was in line with his words about the women in Samaria and his judgement against men who oppressed the poor, *"they trample on the heads of the poor"* (2:7). Yet here they were, bringing their sacrifices and boasting about the size of their freewill offerings, but there was no sincerity in them – their offerings were not acceptable to God.

These words of Amos are fully in line with the words of Isaiah which would no doubt have been known by Amos. Isaiah wrote a direct word from God condemning the meaningless offerings brought by the people. *"Even if you offer many prayers I will not listen. Your hands are full of blood . . . Stop doing wrong, learn to do right! Seek justice, encourage the oppressed. Defend the cause of the fatherless, plead the case of the widow"* (Is 1:15-17). Both prophets were more committed to pursuing justice than carrying out the correct religious ritual.

The central drive in the ministry of Amos was to expose hypocrisy and oppression by those who held power in the nation, and to encourage a right relationship with God.

12 WARNINGS IGNORED   Amos 4:6-11

"I gave you empty stomachs in every city and lack of bread in every town, yet you have not returned to me," declares the Lord.

Five-times, Amos uses the phrase, "*Yet you have not returned to me declares the Lord.*" This is the continuing refrain from a small series of examples of problems or catastrophes that had happened in the recent past. All of these were incidents that God had either directly or indirectly sent as warning signs to the people of Israel. Their purpose was to show the people that something was wrong, and that they needed to seek the Lord for an understanding of what he was saying to them.

This passage of Scripture is fully in line with the concept of the 'sovereignty of God' that was held by all the writing prophets of Israel whereby everything that happens has either been allowed or directed by God. This series of events described by Amos were mostly things that had happened in the world of nature.

The first was a shortage of food. *"I gave you cleanness of teeth in all your cities"* (KJV) which is a right translation but, of course, the clean teeth are simply a metaphor for saying that they had got no food to eat. In the second example a shortage of food was caused by the failure of harvest due to a lack of rain when the seed was sown so that it did not germinate. The rainfall was withheld from some areas but not others, but the significance of this was not noticed by the people.

There was no seeking the Lord for what he was saying to them through this natural event. This is strange because there clearly had been prophets of Yahweh who could have interpreted situations as they occurred. There are references to unnamed prophets as well as outstanding men such as Micaiah who was summoned by Jehoshaphat when he was not sure that all the prophets in Israel were genuine men of God prophesying the truth.

The account in 1 Kings 22 and 2 Chronicles 18 shows that there were plenty of men who were claiming to be prophets, so there would have been no shortage of men offering interpretations of natural phenomena. The fact noted in these examples given by Amos is not that nobody noticed the significance of each event, but that they had all been ignored, *"Yet you have not returned to me,"* declares the Lord.

Amos is not complaining that there is a shortage of men of God who speak the word of truth to the people and who are rightly interpreting the signs of the times. Amos is declaring that in the face of all the different events that have taken place recently no one had taken in the warning signs that something was wrong in these towns and cities.

It was very similar to the sort of situation that in New Testament times Jesus said that people were well able to look at the sky and forecast the weather – it was going to rain, or it would be hot – but they were quite unable to interpret the signs of the times that God had sent to them (Lk 12:54).

This was the complaint that Amos was making: that the people were ignoring all the warning signs that God sent to them to say that something was wrong in the nation. Amos moved from events in nature to other things – a plague like the one God sent when the people were in Egypt – and he was sending powerful warnings, like the warnings he sent to Pharaoh to let the people go. A similar plague had hit the people of Israel in recent times, which some of them might remember.

Young men had died in battle – possibly the battle of Ramoth Gilead to which Amos had made reference in his opening statement about the sins of Damascus, when the combined armies of Israel and Judah had been defeated when trying to reclaim land traditionally part of Israel just south of the Sea of Galilee. Clearly, that had been a terrible tragedy for the people who had been devastated by the scale of the destruction, just as the people Sodom and Gomorrah had been dismayed.

But in the face of this disaster, like the other ones listed by Amos, the warning signs that God was removing his protection from people who were not behaving righteously, all these signs were being ignored. This was the reason for the mission of Amos. In God's great love for his chosen he would go to any lengths, warning them of the danger they faced, calling them to repent and turn back to him so that they could be in a right relationship and come under his loving protection.

13 PREPARE TO MEET GOD   Amos 4:12-13

Therefore this is what I will do to you, Israel, and because I will do this to you prepare to meet your God O Israel.

The words *"Prepare to meet your God O Israel"* would have struck fear into all those who heard Amos. There was a natural fear of meeting God that went right back in the history of Israel. Moses encountered God at the burning bush and was told not to come any closer and to take off his sandals because he was standing on holy ground (Ex 3:5). When Moses came down from the mountain with the Ten Commandments the people stayed at a distance saying, *"Speak to us yourself and we will listen. But do not have God speak to us or we will die"* (Ex 20:19).

Amos was using this fear of God to emphasise the message he was trying to convey the people. The message was not from him, but he was delivering the word of the God of Creation who formed the mountains and sent wind and rain – God Almighty. It was God who had revealed to Amos his thoughts about the nation of Israel. God's thoughts were not the same as those of human beings, as Isaiah had said, *"For my thoughts are not your thoughts, neither are my ways your ways, declares the Lord"* (Is 55:8).

The reason Amos had been sent by God was to warn the people of Israel of impending disaster if they continued along the path they were travelling. He had begun by speaking about the way the rich were oppressing the poor. He had singled out the women in Samaria who were lounging in their sumptuous households and enjoying the wealth produced through injustice, unaware of the danger facing them. He had gone to Bethel and seen the multitude of their sacrifices and heard the men boasting about their freewill offerings, but none of this would save them from the tragedy that lay ahead.

The reason for their blindness was that they did not know the thoughts of God. Isaiah had encountered the same blindness whereby the people thought they had only got to offer ritual sacrifices, and they would be all right despite their hands being full of blood and their ways being unjust. God would not even listen to their prayers

(Is 1:15-17). God's thoughts would turn their worldly values upside down.

Jeremiah encountered the same problems with the people of Jerusalem who thought they were safe because God would always protect them. Jeremiah told them that they were trusting in deceptive words and that they needed to reform their ways and their actions. Their trust was in the temple, but not in God. He spoke of their crimes of injustice, oppression and violence which were part of their lifestyle in society. In spiritual terms they were heavily into idolatry. He said there were idols of foreign gods on every street in Jerusalem and all the family were involved – from adults to children: *"The children gather wood, the fathers light the fire, and the women knead the dough and make cakes of bread for the Queen of Heaven"* (Jer 7:18).

In his famous 'Temple Sermon' – preached from the steps in front of the temple from which he was forbidden by the priests – Jeremiah outlined the sins of the people and then concluded with the solemn warning, *"But I have been watching! declares the Lord"* (Jer 7:11). Amos, in much the same way had spoken both in Samaria and at Bethel about the things that he had personally witnessed. He had also recounted things that happened in the world of nature that should have been interpreted as spiritual warnings. But the people were blind: their social values as well as their spiritual practices were grossly at fault. They were not in line with the thoughts and values of God. Amos had come with a message of warning from God, and this would be the last warning that God would give. This is why he was telling the people to prepare to meet their God who was the Lord of hosts.

Jeremiah spent 40 years of his life trying to convey truth to the people of Judah and the citizens of Jerusalem, but they had not listened. God had graciously sent warning after warning, but there would come a point when the last warning was given and there would be no more. This was why Jeremiah was told three times to stop praying for the welfare of the people (Jer 7:16, 11:14 and 14:11).

The words of Amos here were similarly warning that this was the last opportunity for repentance that was being given to the people. The messenger could do no more. If the people failed to heed the warnings, they would be left to face the consequences without the protection of God.

14 A LAMENT FOR ISRAEL   Amos 5:1-17

Hear this word, O house of Israel, this lament I take up concerning you.

This is a traditional dirge, or lamentation, such as was regularly used in mourning the dead. Ezekiel used a lot of dirges in his prophecies concerning the Gentile nations such as Tyre, where he mourned the destruction of Tyre that had not yet happened, but in Amos it is spoken in the past tense as though it had already happened. The dirge would often be sung, as no doubt it would have been by Ezekiel who had a beautiful voice (Ezek 33:32*). "You say, O Tyre, I am perfect in beauty. Your domain was on the high seas; your builders brought your beauty to perfection*" (Ezek 27:3-4).

The dirge in Hebrew was usually in the form of rhyme or parallelism. Hence, we have in Amos 5:2

> Fallen is virgin Israel
> Never to rise again

Most commentators think that the words *"virgin Israel"* mean that the nation of Israel is already like a fallen woman – she had lost her purity through idolatry. But 'virgin' could also mean a young woman who had never been married, and both cities and nations were often referred to using the feminine case. So, Amos may have been simply referring to the northern kingdom of Israel being a young nation. In fact, Israel only lasted 200 years from the time of the revolt against Rehoboam in 922 BC to the destruction of Samaria by the Assyrians in 722.

Israel was still a young nation when they were wiped off the map of the world, never to rise again. As Amos rightly said, *"There was no-one to lift her up."* God had sent many warnings to the people of Israel over that 200-year period, but none had been heeded and Amos knew that the time would come when God would remove his cover of protection which would lead to disaster. He had come to bring the last warning to a nation basking in prosperity and feeling secure that their army, of which Jeroboam II boasted, was capable of defeating any enemy.

Amos knew that their confidence was false. The city fortresses in which they trusted would each be left with just a small remnant. The only hope for Israel was in repentance and seeking the Lord. It was no use going to Bethel, or Gilgal where they worshipped the golden calf, or even going right down south to worship at Beersheba. It was, of course, highly unlikely anyone from the North would go that far outside their national territory, so this may have been said in irony. Bethel was never rebuilt after the Assyrians destroyed it in 722 BC.

Amos then turned from false religion to the corrupt social values that he saw everywhere, turning justice and righteousness upside down. The God of creation who launched the planets, created the beautiful star constellations, was no other than Yahweh the God of Israel. He who created night and day would send destruction upon even the most heavily guarded cities and bring them to ruin.

Amos returned to the scene with which he had begun his review of the nation of Israel, "*You hate the one who reproves in court and despise him who tells the truth.*" This sounds as though he was talking about a law court, but the Hebrew word for 'court' could equally be translated 'gate' – in other words referring to the council of elders who sat at the city gate dealing with minor infringements or disputes in the community. Amos was scathing in his condemnation of those who had built stone mansions and lived in luxury. This is central in his message, "*Seek good, not evil, that you may live. Then the Lord God Almighty will be with you, just as you say he is.*"

They were convinced that God was with them, but God hated the injustice and the bribery and corruption he saw everywhere in Israel where they bribed the judges and deprived the poor of justice. Amos called upon the people to "*hate evil, love good; maintain justice*" and then perhaps the Lord God Almighty would have mercy. The alternative was that if they stayed pursuing their present way of life regardless of injustice, disaster was inevitable.

Amos foresaw so much horror and cries of anguish that there would not be sufficient mourners (professional singers) to raise a dirge for the Lord. They would have to summon ordinary people like farmers to come and do the wailing, because they had received their last warning. The word of the Lord was that Yahweh, the God of Israel was coming to sweep through the land. They would have to face the judgement of God. His word was, "*I will pass through your midst, says the Lord.*"

15 THE DAY OF THE LORD   Amos 5:18-20

Woe to you who long for the day of the Lord! Why do you long for the day of the Lord? That day will be darkness, not light.

This is one of the most important words in all the writing prophets of Israel. It is a landmark in the history of Israel and in its theological development. Amos is the first to use the phrase *"the day of the Lord"*. He had just made the statement that God was going to come sweeping through the land of Israel in judgement upon the sinfulness of the people. Now he adds that *'the day of the Lord'* would be a day of darkness and not of light as the people expected.

This statement implies that there was a widespread expectation among the people that God was going to do something greatly to the benefit of the people of Israel. They were longing for that day which would fulfil their hopes and dreams. They had forgotten the covenant responsibilities. They were confident that God was on their side, blessing them with great prosperity – good harvests and wonderful new trade routes – bringing wealth into the country which they saw as the signs of God's blessing.

Amos' words must have come as a great shock. Of course, they had been delighted when he had gone through the neighbouring Gentile nations listing their sins, but when he turned the searchlight upon them and began exposing injustice, oppression, and crimes against humanity, they were mortified and angry.

Amos' declaration now that God had fixed a day when he was going to judge the sins of *all* people was a new concept in Israel (although hinted at in verses like Gen 9:5) – certainly a new emphasis in their understanding of God. He was the God who had created the universe, who had created night and day, and he was the God who had chosen the people of Israel to be his people. In the folk religion of Israel everything that happened to them was within his purposes. It was God who had brought them out of Egypt. He gave the land of Canaan to them and overthrew the previous occupants.

The people, however, in the time of Amos did not think of their God as having any jurisdiction over other lands. It was Isaiah who, although a contemporary of Amos and exercising his ministry in Jerusalem, was the first to embrace the universality of the God of creation. Amos was developing something similar in Samaria. He was convinced that God was a God of justice who hated oppression by the powerful over the powerless. He said judgement would come upon the people of Samaria who cared nothing for the poor and who would go to any lengths of bribery and corruption to increase their wealth. In fact, he was so certain of what he was hearing from God that he gave the analogy of a man escaping from a lion, only to meet a bear, and when he got away from him into the safety of his house, he was bitten by a poisonous snake. This was the inevitability of judgement coming upon the people of Samaria.

Isaiah in Jerusalem may have been developing Amos' words: *"The Lord Almighty has a day in store for all the proud and lofty, for all that is exalted . . . The arrogance of man will be brought low, and the pride of men humbled; the Lord alone will be exalted in that day . . . when he rises to shake the nations"* (Is 2:12-19). Isaiah spelt out the principles of God's judgement, *"The Lord Almighty will be exalted by his justice, and the holy God will show himself holy by his righteousness"* (Is 5:16).

Both Jeremiah and Ezekiel, a century later, built upon this concept of God. Jeremiah saw the New Covenant as a new relationship with God through which everyone would know him; and Ezekiel developed the concept of the faithful remnant of believers. This paved the way for the Messianic concept of a 'community of believers' to which Ezekiel added that God himself would make an atonement by cleansing and forgiveness to enable human beings to bridge the gap with the holiness of God.

In Samaria the people were looking forward to 'the day of the Lord' thinking that it was a great day of celebration like the Feast of Tabernacles. Everyone rejoiced on that day when the harvest was gathered in. The rich especially rejoiced to see their barns filled with what would feed them and their families, providing them with wealth and high social status among their neighbours.

Amos declared that they had got it all wrong, and far from being a day of rejoicing, *'the day of the Lord'* would be one of darkness and not light. It would be judgement and not blessing. This was a new understanding of God for the people of Israel.

16 RELIGIOUS SACERDOTALISM   Amos 5:21-27

I hate, I despise your religious feasts, I cannot stand your assemblies. Even though you bring me burnt offerings and grain offerings, I will not accept them.

Amos had already spoken about the religious practices of the people of Israel. He had condemned the activities at Bethel and Gilgal and said that the altars of Bethel would be destroyed. He had seen the elaborate ritual of sacrifices at Bethel, and he had heard the people bragging about the large freewill offerings they had given. In the passage we are studying today, Amos no longer speaks his own words, but he brings a direct word from God.

"I hate, I despise your religious feasts" – nothing could be a more clear denunciation! If God refuses to accept the worship of his people, this is the clearest indication that something is terribly wrong. There follows the famous declaration of Amos that is widely quoted, especially by those who do not like any form of religious ceremonial. But what Amos is saying is not necessarily a condemnation of all religious ceremony but that it must be accompanied by justice and righteousness in community relationships!

Amos was not alone in describing God's aversion to the sacrifices of his people. Isaiah said something similar about animal sacrifice. *"I have more than enough of burnt offerings . . . I have no pleasure in the blood of bulls and lambs and goats . . . Even if you offer many prayers I will not listen"* (Is 1:11-15). In the same passage Isaiah also called for justice and expressed God's hatred of oppression which matched Amos's famous statement, *"Let justice roll on like a river, righteousness like a never-failing stream!"*

It is hard to be sure in either passage whether or not God was dismissing all animal sacrifice and its associated worship with singing and music, or if this was because the worshippers came from a background of violence, injustice and oppression, with blood on their hands.

All the preexilic prophets say something on this subject. Hosea 6:6 says, *"I desire mercy, not sacrifice, and acknowledgement of God rather than burnt offerings."* Jeremiah speaks of God not only speaking to those he brought out of Egypt about offerings and sacrifices, but about their behaviour and the necessity of walking in the ways he commanded (Jer 7:21f). This same discussion of 'faith and works' occurs in the New Testament where Paul speaks of salvation by faith alone and James emphasises the need for good works. One thing that can be said for certain is that the prophets of Israel all agree that religious ceremony alone does not offer salvation. They roundly condemn all forms of sacerdotalism.

It is the following three verses, 25-27 that cause great difficulty for biblical scholars, largely due to the difficulties in translating the Hebrew text where there are several words that only occur here and nowhere else in the Bible. It begins with what appears to be a question, *"Did you bring me sacrifices and offerings for forty years in the desert?"*

This demands the answer, "no"; but was Amos really saying that sacrifices are not necessary? The difficulty lies in the Hebrew that could be read as a question or in the future tense which would lead into verses 26 and 27 where they can be read as a statement that the people of Israel will go into exile and take with them some things for worship, as sacrifices would not be possible in exile.

Verse 25 is very difficult which is why there are widely different translations in different versions of the Bible. The KJV says: *"You have borne the tabernacles of your Molech and Chiun your images the star of your god, ye made to yourselves."* Whereas the NIV says: *"You have lifted up the shrine of your king, the pedestal of your idols, the star of your god – which you made for yourselves."* The NRSV says: *"You shall take up Sukkuth your king, and Kaiwan your star-god, your images, which you made for yourselves."*

This wide diversity in translation shows the difficulty of knowing what Amos was saying here. This is what we referred to in the Introduction where we looked at difficulties that arose with the original Hebrew that had no vowel symbols. The vowels were not put in until well into the Christian era and different rabbis differed in their choice which gave a wide divergence of translations.

The NIV, which we are using in this study, refers to the shrine on which Yahweh stood at Bethel. This was a golden calf, and the pedestal plus the star was probably a star sign on the king's emblem that he carried into battle. All these symbols would be taken with the people when they went into "*exile beyond Damascus*" (to Assyria). They were all useless.

17 FALSE COMPLACENCY   Amos 6:1-7

Woe to you who are complacent in Zion, and to you who feel secure on Mount Samaria, you notable men of the foremost nation, to whom the people of Israel come!

In chapter 6 Amos returns to the theme he expressed in chapter 4 where he gave a strong warning to the women of Samaria against complacency. In this passage the warnings are widened to include the whole nation, both those in the northern kingdom and in the south, both Israel and Judah. The use of 'Zion' instead of Jerusalem is somewhat strange as it usually refers to the religious leaders rather than political leaders, but clearly the charge of complacency is being levelled at both the northern and southern kingdoms.

The leaders in the fortified stronghold on Mount Samaria felt secure because Jeroboam II had built up a powerful army with watchtowers and fortresses that the people believed could withstand attack from any enemy. Similarly, the people in Jerusalem felt secure because Zion was the dwelling place of God. They had the temple, and they were the covenant people enjoying the security of the promises of God. The reference to the *"foremost nation"* could, of course, have been sarcasm – but as Amos himself was from Judah he was well aware of the religious heritage of the people of Israel as the chosen people of God, which may have been the reason why he spoke here of Zion rather than Jerusalem.

The charge of complacency, however, applied to both kingdoms. The people in Samaria trusted in the strength of their army and fortifications whereas the people in Jerusalem falsely trusted God would protect them under all circumstances regardless of their behaviour. The instruction to go to Calneh, Hamath and Gath is something that biblical scholars find difficult to explain. There appears to be no obvious link, and Amos could not have been referring to their destruction because he was prophesying about the year 750 BC whereas Calneh and Hamah were not destroyed until 738 BC and Gath was not destroyed until 711 BC. All three of them were, however, cities in decline during Amos' lifetime. Calneh on the banks of the River Tigris had been the capital city of the Assyrian

Empire but had now lost its status. Hamath and Gath were also cities in decline and Amos may have simply been warning that even the most prominent cities have no lasting value.

The main warning here is against complacency. In Samaria the people were undoubtedly lounging in luxury, eating the finest food and enjoying a lifestyle of wanton self-indulgence, totally unaware of the dangers that lay ahead of which Amos had been sent to warn them. This warning equally applied to the southern kingdom of Judah where the people also had a false sense of security. By going to see the renowned cities of the Gentiles that were now in decay, the people of Israel might have been made to recognise that they were no better than anyone else. Amos was clearly looking for anything that might be effective in shaking the people out of their dangerous complacency.

The phrase in verse 3, *"You put off the evil day and bring near a reign of terror"* is difficult to understand because it has words in the Hebrew text that are not repeated elsewhere. This is the reason for the different translations in other versions of the Bible. The KJV says, *"Ye that put far away the evil day, and cause the seat of violence to come near."* The NRSV says, *"O you that put far away the evil day, and bring near a reign of violence."* The difficult words here are *nadah*, meaning 'to remove' or 'cast out'; *nagash* means 'to put away', and *chamas* is violence or oppression. This verse has provoked a great deal of discussion among biblical scholars, but there is no agreement on exactly what it does mean.

Some scholars link this verse with the Feast of Tabernacles when the last day was known as the 'Day of the Enthronement of the Lord'. Amos' message was that a great day of the Lord will not be a day of light but a day of darkness and judgement. So, this verse is interpreted as meaning that people had turned upside down the message of God by their eating and drinking at the feast, but they had not enthroned Yahweh. So, they had actually brought nearer the day of darkness and violence upon themselves.

There was no repentance – only feasting and drinking by the bowlful, so they did not see the true situation in the nation and the threat to the very existence of the Northern Kingdom of Israel that would be the first to go into exile. The final phrase in verse 7, *"Your feasting and lounging will end"* would turn their joy into a funeral dirge for the nation.

18 THE PRIDE OF ISRAEL   Amos 6:8-14

The Sovereign Lord has sworn by himself – the Lord God Almighty declares: "I abhor the pride of Jacob and detest his fortresses; I will deliver up the city and everything in it."

In this passage Amos launched a devastating attack upon the pride of Israel. He declared that it was God himself who hated the pride of the nation and its false belief in its own military strength – a particular feature of Jeroboam II's reign. He took a great interest in building up the military might of the nation, and he established fortresses in all the major towns around the land. He took special interest in Samaria which was on high ground that formed a natural defensive protection against invasion together with its watchtowers and walls.

Jeroboam had evidently recently retaken some territory in the Gilead area of northern Israel and there was widespread rejoicing among the people which Amos saw as a direct insult to God's name which had not been mentioned. All the honour and glory had been given to Jeroboam and his army.

Amos said that God was going to deliver Israel into the hands of a powerful enemy who would overcome even the strongest defences of Samaria which were the pride of Jacob. God detested this pride which ignored God and gave all the glory to human beings. The God of Israel would withdraw his protection and open the way for the enemy to devastate the land.

The illustration given in verses 9 and 10 has puzzled biblical scholars for many generations. The most usual interpretation is that the 'ten men' are a small military unit who had withdrawn to their base where the enemy had entered and killed them all. A relative came to bury them, but first enquired if anyone was still alive. The answer was 'no' so all the bodies had to be burnt. There was no explanation given for this: cremation was not practised in Israel, so there had to be a special reason. It is usually thought that there must have been an outbreak of plague, but no one can be certain.

There is also uncertainty over the reason why nobody should mention the name of the Lord. Probably the best explanation is that there was no point in calling upon the name of Yahweh for help as it was he who had given the command to the enemy that they were free to destroy the people of Israel and to smash their houses, great or small.

The reason why God had withdrawn his cover of protection was not only because he hated the pride of Israel but because they had turned justice upside down. This is what lies behind the little illustration of horses galloping over rocky ground or trying to plough it. The leaders of the nation who had become rich and powerful at the expense of the poor and powerless had turned justice into poison which had contaminated the whole of society. There was no righteousness in the land so that community relationships were poisonous.

The whole value system of the nation was corrupted because they had turned their backs upon God. They were rejoicing in having retaken a bit of land on the north-eastern outskirts of Israel, but in God's sight it was of no significance. The two towns named here, 'Lo Debar' and 'Karnaim' are probably not actual towns, but these names are simply used as puns, meaning that they are of no great significance – they are as nothing, of no value. In Hebrew *Lo Debar* was a well-known term for 'nothing'. It was just an idiom used in a dismissive manner. If someone was boasting about something trivial it could be dismissed as rubbish – '*Lo Debar*'. Similarly *Karnaim*, which literally meant 'horns', was a symbol of power. So put together, the phrase meant that it had no substance – it was just rubbish.

There are two towns of these names mentioned in the earlier history of Israel, but there is no certainty as to their location. Karnaim occurs in Genesis 14:5 and Lo Debar is found in 2 Samuel 9:4-5 and 17:27, but we do not know where they were, or if there is any significance in their names. The most probable use here by Amos is in an idiomatic sense.

Amos ends this passage with a direct prophecy that Yahweh the God of Israel was about to act in judgement of the injustice and oppression he saw among his people. God was going to allow their enemy to exercise judgement upon them from one end of the country to the other, from North to South. Judgement would fall upon the whole land of Israel. Their enemies would "*oppress you all the way from Lobo Hamath to the valley of the Arabah.*"

19 LOCUSTS AND FIRE   Amos 7:1-6

This is what the Sovereign Lord showed me: he was preparing swarms of locusts after the king's share had been harvested and just as the second crop was coming up.

This is said at the beginning of a lengthy passage where Amos lists a number of visions. These are recounted from the beginning of chapter 7 through to 9:10. These are not presented as part of the public ministry of Amos, but they are simply recorded as personal experiences. The first three visions in 7:1-8 and others in 8:1-3, are interrupted by the account of Amos meeting with Amaziah the priest at Bethel.

The first vision is about the purposes of God. There are many references to locusts in the Bible and the devastating effect that they can have in stripping every vestige of vegetation from the land. A plague of locusts was sent against Egypt where they would *"cover the face of the ground so that it cannot be seen"* (Ex 10:4). A swarm of locusts was one of the most feared events that could happen in an agricultural community. It would involve millions of the creatures who seem to spring up from the ground which is the literal meaning of the Hebrew word *gov* (locust) which comes from the verb *govah* – literally *"to come up out of the earth"*.

In this vision Amos sees a swarm of locusts covering the ground and eating everything just as the spring crop was coming up in the fields. This would have been the crop of wheat which was the main source of food for the people. It followed the barley harvest which was usually first and was used mainly for cattle feed, or for very coarse cheap food, barley bread, for the poor.

The phrase here that the king's share had already been harvested is very unclear. The Hebrew literally reads *"after the king's mowing"* which is how it is translated in the KJV and NRSV.

This may mean that it was a crop of hay that was mown and given for the king's horses following a long dry summer and a hard winter. It does not necessarily mean that there would be a second harvest. It may mean that this was some form of tax – the first fruit of the harvest which went to the king. After this the farmers could have the main harvest for the people. There is no agreement among biblical scholars as to the precise meaning of these words, either the identity of the "king's share" or the "second crop". The threat from a swarm of locusts, however, is very clear.

In this first vision Amos sees the locusts stripping the land clean and he knows that this means starvation for all the poor who depended upon that harvest. He cried out to God to forgive the sins of the people, saying, *"How can Jacob survive? He is so small!"* The meaning of the smallness of Jacob is unclear. It may not mean small in the sense of size but in terms of significance, or ability to survive a time of famine that would result from a swarm of locusts destroying all vegetation.

Amos uses the term 'Jacob' rather than 'Israel'. It may be that this vision was given to Amos at Bethel which was the place where Jacob had his dream and became a changed man (Gen 28:10-19). Amos was looking for a major change in the people of Israel which was the objective of his prophetic ministry to the northern kingdom.

In the second vision given to Amos he saw a great fire that was going to devour the whole land. Once again Amos interceded on behalf of the people, crying out, *"Sovereign Lord, I beg you, stop! How can Jacob survive? He is so small!"* The judgement that was being threatened here was that fire would sweep across the countryside devouring the land and that there would be no rain to quench the fire. The land would be dried up, resulting in a great drought that would produce famine.

This is what is threatened here rather than the forthcoming invasion of the Assyrians burning towns and villages. Indeed, that did not happen, but rather the Assyrians took whole populations from Israel and replaced them with people from other parts of their empire to occupy the vacant properties in towns of Israel.

The threat of drought drying up all vegetation is threatened in the second vision and again Amos intercedes, and God relents. In this vision Amos does not say that God forgives the people, but he relents from sending this judgement. This is an important development in the presentation of the nature and purposes of God given through Amos. God is seen as showing mercy as a pure act of unmerited grace.

20 THE PLUMB-LINE OF THE LORD   Amos 7:7-9

This is what he showed me: the Lord was standing by a wall that had been built true to plumb, with a plumbline in his hand. And the Lord asked me, "What do you see, Amos?"

In this third vision Amos is shown a scene that would have been fairly familiar to people in any of the walled cities of Israel at that time, except that in Amos' vision it is the Lord whom he sees standing with a plumbline in his hand. This comes as a shock to Amos. He reacts immediately when the Lord makes it clear what he is saying.

The plumbline was an instrument widely used in the building industry in the same way as it is used today. It is simply a metal weight tied on the end of a piece of string. Anyone who has tried home decoration will have used a plumbline in hanging wallpaper to ensure that it is upright. In Amos' day every walled city had an engineer or a surveyor whose task was regularly to check the safety of the walls. Most city walls in those days were composed of an outer and inner wall with the cavity filled with rubble often mixed with the city rubbish. If this decomposed it would expand and the corruption inside the wall would build up the pressure and cause a bulge. This bulge would be detected by the surveyor using a plumbline from the top of the wall.

A failure to detect the corruption in a wall could cause a sudden collapse which could be catastrophic. There is a remarkable similarity between what Amos was seeing and the message of Isaiah, *"Because you have rejected this message, relied on oppression and depended on deceit, this sin will become for you like a high wall, cracked and bulging, that collapses suddenly, in an instant"* (Is 30:12-14). Isaiah knew that the safety of the citizens depended upon the strength of the city's walls when there was danger of an attack from an enemy. The walls had to be sound, not cracked and bulging, or they could easily be destroyed.

In the same way God would not protect a city where the people were full of violence, oppression, and deceitful sins. The moral and spiritual corruption in that city was similar to the physical corruption inside the walls that would cause them to bulge and to collapse. Amos had already identified the injustice, oppression, bribery and corruption in the city of Samaria and among its leaders. This, he declared was abhorrent to the Lord God of Israel. He had spoken strongly to the women of Samaria and to the leaders, warning that God would not protect them from the enemy and that they would be taken into exile to a faraway country beyond Damascus.

Jeremiah also brought similar warnings to the people of Jerusalem. He used a clay pot which he smashed in the presence of the elders when he prophesied, *"This is what the Lord Almighty says: I will smash this nation and this city just as this potter's jar is smashed and cannot be repaired"* (Jer 19:10). In a similar way, Amos could see the city of Samaria being smashed despite the huge fortifications installed by Jeroboam.

Amos had spent time going around the market and the streets of Samaria that led to his opening statements about life in Israel where they trampled on the heads of the poor and denied justice to the oppressed. In his first two visions of the judgement that God was planning through a plague of locusts and a great fire, he had pleaded with God for mercy and the Lord had responded, saying, *"This will not happen."* Now in this third vision he says that he saw the Lord standing by a wall that had been built true to plumb with a plumbline in his hand. Amos was no longer pleading for mercy. He heard the Lord say, *"Look, I am setting a plumbline among my people Israel; I will spare them no longer."*

Amos knew that pleading for mercy was useless. He knew that the plumbline of the Lord would reveal the depths of corruption in the city and, as it was God himself who had come to judge his people, Amos knew there could only be one result. He then heard the judgement pronounced, *"I will spare them no longer."* There was no point in asking for mercy now.

All the warnings had been ignored. Bethel with its golden calf and Samaria with its brazen lifestyle and sinful people would have to be destroyed. The word of the Lord was, *"With my sword I will rise against the house of Jeroboam."* God himself would use the Assyrians to exercise judgement upon his people.

21 AMOS AND AMAZIAH   Amos 7:10-17

Then Amaziah the priest of Bethel sent a message to Jeroboam king of Israel: "Amos is raising a conspiracy against you in the very heart of Israel. The land cannot bear all his words."

We are not told where Amos was when he received the three visions that have just been described in chapter 7, but as they are followed by the encounter with Amaziah we may assume that he was at Bethel. We also do not know whether any of them were presented publicly or if they were confined to his private thoughts. The third vision, however, appears to be a statement that was delivered publicly as a prophecy, which could well account for the outburst from Amaziah.

The reference to the "*high places of Isaac*" being destroyed is a mystery and most biblical scholars believe it to be a scribal error, and that originally 'Isaac' would have been 'Jacob'. There does not appear to have been any reason for the inclusion of Isaac, but Amos' following statement that *"the sanctuaries of Israel will be ruined"* is a direct verbal attack upon Bethel. This was followed by the statement that the sword of the Lord would be raised against the house of Jeroboam.

This could not be ignored by Amaziah. He reacted in anger by sending a message to the king accusing Amos of what amounted to treason. The statement *"Amos is raising a conspiracy against you in the very heart of Israel"* would surely have brought a reaction from Jeroboam whose household was politically insecure, although he himself had been on the throne for 40 years and had established his authority. As soon as Jeroboam died, however, his son Zechariah succeeded him, but he only lasted six months before he was assassinated by Shallum, who himself was assassinated only one month later. Clearly it was a very unstable time for the monarchy in Samaria according to its history set out in 2 Kings 14 – 17.

Amaziah would have known about the political undercurrent in Samaria, hence his warning about Amos raising 'a conspiracy'. This would have been the quickest way to get a reaction from Samaria, especially when he followed it by reporting some of Amos' words saying that Jeroboam would die, and Israel would go into exile.

Amaziah then addressed Amos directly, ordering him to get out of Israel and go back to the land of Judah.

This whole incident is about the question of authority. Amaziah was the duly appointed priest at Bethel. He was what sociologists know as an 'institutional functionary', and the only one with the authority to make pronouncements at the king's sanctuary. It was therefore quite understandable that he should challenge the authority of this man from Judah. Amos' answer – that he was not a prophet – is not an act of humility, but a simple statement of fact. He did not hold any recognised appointment in Jerusalem. He had no ascribed status by birth, or priestly appointment. He was just a farmer, but his authority was the call of Yahweh upon his life.

There has been a lot of speculation as to what this claim to be a shepherd really meant. Was Amos really just a humble shepherd tending the flock, or was he a wealthy farmer owning a large estate? The answer is that we do not know. We simply have to accept what Amos himself testifies, that his authority came from God. Of course, anyone can make such a claim. It was Moses who gave us a definition of 'the prophet' through the arrangement with his brother Aaron (Ex 4:15-16 and 7:1). Moses also warned about false prophets (Deut 13). Later, Ezekiel had to deal with false 'prophets' in Babylon (Ezek 13) as Jeremiah had to deal with the false prophet Hananiah (Jer 28).

Amaziah was justified in questioning Amos's right to be a prophet. He was the appointed religious authority. God had called Amos saying, *"Go, prophesy to my people Israel."* This was **his** authority. He had not come to Samaria or Bethel on his own authority or any human being. His words were those of the God of Israel. Therefore, Amaziah was speaking against God in telling him not to prophesy against Israel.

The authority of God over human beings, or governments, or institutions, has always been questioned. Jesus had to face the same question when he drove the cattle out of the temple and overturned the moneychangers' tables.

Amos then gave a devastating judgement upon the people of Israel and upon Amaziah personally. He said that Israel would certainly go into exile away from their native country, and that Amaziah personally would lose his own land and then die in exile. His wife would stay in the city but her status would be so reduced that she would resort to harlotry for survival.

22 THE BASKET OF RIPE FRUIT Amos 8:1-6

This is what the Sovereign Lord showed me: a basket of ripe fruit. "What do you see, Amos?" he asked. "A basket of ripe fruit," I answered.

This is the fourth vision that Amos was given. He saw a basket of summer fruit. This may not have begun as a vision, but something that he actually saw, possibly for sale in the market. Seeing the basket of fruit, he heard the Lord say to him, *"What do you see Amos?"* And he said, *"A basket of ripe fruit"*, to which the Lord responded, *"The time is ripe for my people Israel."* This would have been at the end of the agricultural year – late August or early September and the fruit would have been grapes or olives or figs which were usually the last fruit to be harvested.

In order to understand the message being conveyed to Amos we have to look at the play upon words involved here. There are two puns in this exchange of words. The word *qayis* (pronounced ka-yi-tz) means 'summer fruit', or 'end of the year fruit'. The second pun was with the word *qetz* which means 'the end', but it sounds very similar to 'summer fruit.' So the two words were put together in the response from God to what Amos was seeing. This produced the response, *"The time is ripe for my people Israel: I will spare them no longer."*

There are strong similarities here with the baskets of fruit placed in front of the temple that Jeremiah saw more than a century later. The fruit were figs, which marked the end of the season. Some were ready for eating; others were beginning to rot and were only fit for throwing away. The figs led Jeremiah to receive a word from the Lord about the people who had been taken into exile in Babylon. They were good fruit who would be preserved whereas those remaining in Jerusalem were beyond redemption (Jer 24). It is very possible that Jeremiah had read Amos' word.

The puns between God and Amos were similar to those employed in the earliest conversation recorded between God and Jeremiah. Jeremiah was asked the question, *"What do you see?"* (Jer 1:11). He was looking at an almond tree which sounded like the Hebrew verb 'to watch', which led to God saying that he was watching to see his word fulfilled. In the words to Amos, God declared that he would no longer spare the people of Israel from judgement.

"In that day, declares the Sovereign Lord, the songs in the temple will turn to wailing." It is strange that the temple should be brought into this word which was addressed to the people of Israel, the northern kingdom where Amos was ministering, although there is some support for the word 'palace' rather than 'temple', which would be more appropriate here. The point being made is that those who now were singing their riotous songs of pleasure in the palace of Jeroboam would soon find their rejoicing turning to mourning. The picture of death and destruction is terrifying, with bodies flung everywhere, the sound of wailing – followed by silence – the silence of death. This is the scene that Amos was foreseeing in the coming of the Assyrians. They would break through the defences of Samaria and destroy the city, slaughtering its citizens without mercy, leaving the ruins empty and silent.

This prophecy of judgement when God removed his cover of protection and allowed the Assyrians the freedom to conquer his people is immediately linked here with the social sins of the rich and powerful who cared nothing for the poor and powerless. The sins described were things that Amos had seen in the marketplace of Samaria. He had heard merchants eager for the new moon festivals and Sabbaths to be over so that they could get on with the real business of making money. Amos was not charging the merchants with Sabbath-breaking. They were observing the religious restrictions on work during festivals and Sabbaths, but clearly these times had no spiritual significance for them. Holy days interrupted the important business of commerce during which they cheated and deceived the poor.

Amos had seen their business practices, cheating with dishonest weights on their scales and pushing up the price of wheat. They had no compassion for the poor and they would even sell debtors into slavery. He had even noticed the stall holders in the market sweeping dust with the corn into the housewives' baskets. It was the desire for dishonest gain and the total disregard of those who were powerless, that made Amos angry. He knew that God hates injustice and oppression, and these were the things he saw all around him amidst the affluence and indulgence of the rich who were totally unaware of the danger that faced them.

23 THE PRIDE OF JACOB Amos 8:7-14

The Lord has sworn by the pride of Jacob: "I will never forget anything they have done. Will not the land tremble for this, and all who live in it mourn?"

This is a strange declaration that God would swear by the pride of Jacob. An oath was usually sworn by something fixed and immovable. It may be here that God was referring to the unshakeable pride of Jacob. Despite all the warning signs that had been given to them there was no sign of repentance or turning. In the face of this, God spoke his terrible oath saying that he would never forget the things that had been done by the people of Israel. He was going to shake the land in such a way that everyone trembled, and all their pride would be broken and turn to mourning. This word was said in the context of the basket of ripe fruit which would have been at the Feast of Tabernacles, so what is being said here was that all festivities and joyfulness would be turned into sorrow and mourning.

It would not just be the people whose lives would be shaken, but the whole land would tremble. This foretold some catastrophic event in the world of nature which would be like the rising of the Nile. This is a strange analogy because the fertility of the land of Egypt depended upon the Nile rising by at least 21 feet each year in order to fertilise the land and produce a good harvest. What God was promising was something in which the normal cycle of nature was turned upside down with disastrous results. It would be like the sun going down at noon and darkening the earth. This would turn the feasts into times of mourning and bitterness.

The catastrophic event in nature is not clearly identified but it would be such that the lives of all the people would be affected and their rejoicing would be turned into sorrow and weeping. They would all be wearing sackcloth and shaving their heads as a sign of mourning and bitterness. This has some similarities with what Ezekiel was seeing happen among the exiles in Babylon who would deeply repent of their sinfulness that had brought catastrophe upon Jerusalem – they would *"loathe themselves"* (Ezek 20:43). This was the measure of repentance that would be an outcome of what was going to happen to the people of Israel that would break their pride and bring repentance.

In the second picture in this piece God declares that he will be sending a famine throughout the land of Israel that will not be a famine of food but a famine of the word of God. People will stagger throughout the land looking for the word of the Lord – not being able to understand what was happening. It will be as though the whole world of nature has been turned upside down and people will be desperate to hear from God.

What is happening here is a reference to the lessons that were learned by the people of Israel in the years they spent in the desert. In those days they desperately searched for bread and found none. They had to learn to trust God. In Deuteronomy 8, Moses gave them a command in preparation for them entering the promised land. He said, *"Remember how the Lord your God led you all the way in the desert these forty years, to humble you and to test you in order to know what is in your heart, whether or not you would keep his commands."*

Moses reminded the people how God had fed them with manna – to **humble**, to **test**, and to **teach** them that *"man does not live on bread alone but on every word that comes from the mouth of the Lord"* (Deut 8:1-3).

We do not know how long Amos spent in his mission to the northern kingdom of Israel and whether he went from town to town – from North to South declaring the word of the Lord, but we do know that all his warnings were ignored. In this word he is seeing people *"stagger from sea to sea . . . searching for the word of the Lord but they would not find it."*

In his final statement on the coming day of the Lord, Amos saw young people who had all been brought up to worship the golden calf, the false god of Israel, being dismayed, *"they will fall never to rise again."* This is a terrible pronouncement, but even this did not bring widespread repentance to the people of Israel. Amos must have been feeling desperate. At this point in his ministry after all that he had said, both in Samaria and in Bethel, his warnings were still being ignored.

24 A FINAL WARNING OF DESTRUCTION
Amos 9:1-8a

I saw the Lord standing by the altar, and he said: "Smash the tops of the pillars so that the thresholds shake. Bring them down on the heads of all the people;[1] those who are left I will kill with the sword."

This sounds very much like the incident, well known in the history of Israel, of Samson destroying the temple of Baal bringing death and destruction to all those inside, including himself. This story would have been well known to Amos, but here he sees the Lord standing beside the altar. The big question that biblical scholars have argued about for centuries is the location of Amos. Where was he? Did he see this vision when standing at Bethel, or Samaria, or even in Jerusalem?

Most scholars agree that the evidence points to Bethel. Amos saw God standing by the altar with its golden calf and he heard God giving a command to strike the pillars and bring the whole structure down. This foreshadowed the onslaught of the Assyrian invasion that would overcome Samaria and the whole country of Israel. This command of the Lord opened the way for the destruction of Bethel's idolatrous edifice. It also foreshadowed the slaughter of the leaders of the nation and it painted a terrible picture of destruction. Those who managed to get away when the enemy struck would be pursued wherever they hid. If they went to the top of Mount Carmel or to the coast they would be hunted down.

Even if the people are taken into exile by the enemy, they could no longer expect protection and blessing from God who had now pronounced judgement upon the nation of Israel. *"I will fix my eyes upon them for evil and not for good"* is the terrible pronouncement. This was reinforced by the God of Creation controlling the world of nature that was going to be shaken in the same way as the River Nile rises and falls. God was going to do something in the land of Israel to demonstrate his power. He would call for judgement, and it will fall upon the whole land.

---

[1] "Bring them down . . ." is the author's translation.

The most damning statement in the whole of this section in verse 7 states, "'*Are not you Israelites the same to me as the Cushites?' declares the Lord.*" This is a reversal of the statement that Amos recorded in 3:2, "*You only have I chosen of all the families of the earth.*" The whole family of Israel was in a special relationship with God. That covenant relationship was established at Mount Sinai in the time of Moses. It was on the basis of that covenant that Israel had been given the land they now occupied, and they had enjoyed the blessings of prosperity and the protection of the Lord in every generation.

At the time when the Torah had been given, Moses warned the people that the blessings of God were dependent upon the faithfulness of the people. If they were unfaithful and worshipped other gods, that would be breaking the covenant and serious consequences would follow. Moses had warned that the people would only occupy the land so long as they were faithful in keeping the covenant, but if they were unfaithful, they would be driven from the land and scattered among the nations. In Deuteronomy 30 it is recorded that if God disperses the people among the nations and they turn to him with all their heart and soul: *"Then the Lord your God will restore your fortunes and have compassion on you and gather you again from all the nations where he scattered you . . . He will bring you to the land that belonged to your fathers"* (Deut 30:2-3).

What Amos was now saying was that the sins of Israel were so great that God would no longer regard them as his people in a covenant relationship with him. They were no more than any of the Gentile nations such as the Cushites and the Philistines and the Arameans. He said that the eyes of the Lord were on the sinful nation and that he was now determined to finish his relationship with them. In verse 8a Amos makes the dreadful statement of finality, *"Surely the eyes of the Sovereign Lord are on the sinful kingdom. I will destroy it from the face of the earth."*

In this passage God acknowledges that he brought the people of Israel out of slavery in Egypt, but now he was saying that this was really no different from bringing other nations in other parts of the world. Amos was now declaring that Israel had forfeited its special relationship with God. Their idolatrous practices and corrupt social life of injustice and oppression and the shedding of innocent blood had reached the point where God could no longer tolerate their presence in his land.

25 RESTORATION OF ISRAEL   Amos 9:8b-15

"I will not totally destroy the house of Jacob," declares the Lord. "For I will give the command, and I will shake the house of Israel, among all the nations."

This is not an easy passage to understand because it turns upside down the message that Amos has been giving throughout the book. Many biblical scholars think it looks as though an editor did not like the finality of the statement in verse 8a that God would destroy Israel *"from the face of the earth"* so that sentence was finished with *"yet I will not totally destroy the house of Jacob, declares the Lord."*

Of course, it is possible that Amos himself added this piece as an afterthought. The statement in verses 9 and 10 certainly seems in line with Amos' thinking. The statement that God will shake the house of Israel accords well with the warnings that God had been giving through Amos. It is here applied to the sinners, particularly those who were deliberately opposing the warnings of disaster that Amos brought.

Those who said that *"disaster will not overtake or meet us"* were undermining the truth so that there was no repentance and turning away from the sins that were detestable to God. Amos had been sent with a message of warning which had been rejected by the rich and powerful in Samaria. It had also been rejected by Amaziah the priest in charge of the sanctuary at Bethel. With no repentance in the nation, judgement was inevitable, and Amos clearly believed that God would be fully justified in wiping the nation of Israel off the face of the earth.

The justice of God is, nevertheless, very different from that of human beings and while he would not protect the land from invasion by ruthless enemies, God could find some way of protecting the righteous, even as he did when Jerusalem was about to be destroyed and Ezekiel heard God say, *"Go throughout the city of Jerusalem and put a mark on the foreheads of those who grieve and lament over all the detestable things that are being done in it"* (Ezek 9:4). In a similar way the metaphor of the sieve was to distinguish the good grain from the chaff.

This led to the vision of restoration that the day would come when God would restore *"David's fallen tent"*. This is not a good translation. The KJV says, *"the tabernacle of David"* and the NRSV says, *"the booth of David"* which is literally correct because the Hebrew is *sukkah,* from which we get the plural *Sukkoth* – The Feast of Tabernacles, or Booths. It clearly means the house of David which had been divided since the time of Rehoboam.

The use of the term *'in that day'* clearly refers to God's end time restoration of Israel when the divided house of Israel will be reunited and become one family. This was the vision given to Jeremiah who foresaw the day coming *"when I will bring my people Israel and Judah back from captivity and restore them to the land"* (Jer 30:3).

The promise here in verse 11 to repair broken places, restore ruins and rebuild the house of David is a promise of both physical and spiritual restoration such as Jeremiah perceived when he heard God promise to make a new covenant with the house of Israel and with the house of Judah (Jer 31:31). There are similar promises in other prophets such as, "*I will create Jerusalem to be a delight and its people a joy*" (Is 65:19). Ezekiel received the promise "*they will never again be two nations or be divided*" (Ezek 37:22).

Amos 9:12 sees the restored Israel having borders held under King David including Edom and the whole land from the Jordan to the Mediterranean Sea. Verses 13 and 14 foresee the amazing fertility of the land that will produce abundant fruit so much that the farmers will still be harvesting the last of the crop when the seeds of the next crop are sown. The ruined cities will be rebuilt and vineyards and gardens will produce abundance. The whole house of Israel will be planted back in their land never again to be uprooted. This is the end time vision for Israel that has not yet been fulfilled. It was not fulfilled in the time of Zerubbabel when the people of Judah came back after 537 BC when Cyrus overthrew Babylon, and it was not fulfilled in 1948 when only a tiny parcel of land around Tel Aviv was given to the newly formed state of Israel.

In Ezekiel 39 when the whole world is against Israel, God deals decisively with those who are implacably haters of Israel and God, and Zechariah foresees the day coming when, "*The Lord will be king over the whole earth*" (Zech 14:9). This is what Amos was foreseeing.

CONCLUSION: THE UNIQUE MESSAGE OF AMOS

The central message of Amos is that God is a covenant keeping God. After his opening announcement of God roaring from Zion, he then presents a devastating snapshot review of the Gentile neighbours of Israel, exposing their sins in the name of the God of Israel who is also the one and only God of all nations. We are not told whether this was presented in Samaria or at Bethel, but Amos chose a venue where he could gather a substantial crowd to hear his proclamation which would have undoubtedly been increasingly warmly received, especially when he described the sins of his own tribe of Judah. By this time the crowd would have been hanging on his words with great glee.

It was at this point that Amos turned the searchlight of the word of God upon Israel: *"They sell the righteous for silver, and the needy for a pair of sandals. They trample on the heads of the poor as upon the dust of the ground and deny justice to the oppressed!"* (Am 2:7). Many in the crowd would have been delighted to hear this, but others would have been extremely annoyed. But Amos was in full flow with his message, and he immediately reminded the people of their history declaring that what he was saying was the word of the God who had brought them up out of Egypt and led them for 40 years through the desert. He reminded them that the words he was proclaiming were not new. God had raised up prophets among them over many years, *"sons of Nazirites"* who had been persecuted and the word of God ignored.

But God was a covenant-keeping God! He keeps his promises! God had established a covenant, *"You only have I chosen of all the families of the earth;"* that would have been highly popular with all in the crowd, but then came the punchline: *"Therefore, I will punish you for all your sins!"* (Am 3:2). The covenant was a two-way agreement, that God would always bless the people of Israel, but only if they were faithful to him and worshipped no other God.

If these words were said in Bethel, Amos would have pointed to the great golden calf that was worshipped by the people. If he was in

Samaria, he would have pointed to the Asherah pole that Ahab had set up there. *"Does a lion roar without having any intention of springing upon his prey?"* This was why God had sent him from Jerusalem to declare the word of the Lord. *"On the day I punish Israel for her sins, I will destroy the altars of Bethel"* – and the fine mansions of the rich, he added (Am 3:14).

This was a very different message from that given by the contemporary priests and prophets in Israel who only gave nice words to the people. Amos was declaring that God is a God who keeps his promises because he is a God of justice as well as love. Unless the people of Israel kept their promises of faithfulness to God as part of the covenant relationship, they could not expect God to be patient with them for ever. Amos was sent to declare that the 'day of the Lord' had now come. But that day was not a day of blessing bringing greater prosperity and joy to the people of Israel. The promises of God were that judgement would come upon the people if they continued to be unfaithful and worshipped other gods – that promise was soon to be fulfilled because God was faithful to keep his covenant promises. He was a God of justice as well as love.

INTRODUCTION TO TODAY WITH HOSEA

The Identity of Hosea

We know little about Hosea other than what is revealed in chapters 1 to 3 which focus on his marriage. If it were not for these three chapters, we would know nothing about him. From other chapters we know that his ministry was mainly directed towards the northern kingdom of Israel, but there are also many references to Judah in the south.

From this, most biblical scholars have inferred that unlike the southerner Amos, Hosea was likely to be a native of Israel, sent by God to the north to prophesy in Samaria and Bethel. He also had strong links with Jerusalem where there were hopes of a re-united kingdom and a new era like as under King David and his son Solomon before the break between Rehoboam and Jeroboam I – also to be the vision of King Josiah, a century later.

Hosea was the only one of the eighth century BC prophets who was actually born in Israel which may account for difficulties in translating many words which may be in a different Hebrew dialect. Amos and Micah are more straightforward. The difficulties in the text of Hosea have led to the use of the Septuagint and using the Greek for shedding light on some of the most difficult Hebrew passages.

Historical Background

The historical background to the book of Hosea is essentially the same as that of Amos. Like Amos he ministered in Israel between 750 BC and the end of the century. But unlike Amos, Hosea was a resident of Israel and spoke the local dialect, so he was not a foreigner as Amos was.

The first verse of Hosea tells us that he ministered during *"the reigns of Uzziah, Jotham, Ahaz and Hezekiah, kings of Judah, and the reign of Jeroboam the son of Joash king of Israel."* This is a long period of 56 years if taken from the end of *Uzziah*'s reign in 742 BC to the end of Hezekiah's reign in 687 BC. If just taken to the beginning of Hezekiah's reign it is at least a period of 27 years.

Structure of the Book

Chapters 1 to 3 are very different from the rest, which has led many scholars to leave the study of these three chapters until the end. If we had begun with chapter 4, we would certainly have a very different view of Hosea's teaching, which is even harsher than that found in Amos.

Hosea's teaching focuses upon the sins of Israel and although there are numerous calls to return to the Lord, such as in chapter 6 where there is no sign of repentance and turning, the pronouncements of judgement are continuous with only occasionally statements like *"I desire mercy, not sacrifice, and acknowledgement of God rather than burnt offerings"* (6:6).

The general spirit running right through the book of Hosea is seen in statements such as, *"Do not rejoice, O Israel, do not be jubilant like the other nations. For you have been unfaithful to your God, you love the wages of a prostitute"* (9:1). Hosea foresees the diaspora: *"My God will reject them because they have not obeyed him, they will be wanderers among the nations"* (9:17).

This emphasis upon the sinfulness of the nation, and coming judgement, is amazingly changed in chapter 11. This is where the character of Hosea himself and his relationship with Gomer, detailed in the first three chapters, gives us an incredible insight into the nature of God. He tenderly describes the suffering of God who responded to the cries of Israel enslaved in Egypt. It was God who redeemed the people from slavery, taught them to walk and supported them with *"cords of human kindness"* (Hos 11:4), but they did not respond to the love of God. This presented God with a terrible choice – allow them to suffer devastating judgement or rescue them yet again?

Israel continued in their sins until the last chapter, but always there is the possibility, *"I will ransom them from the power of the grave, I will redeem them from death"* (13:14). This prepares the way for the final chapter where again the emphasis is upon returning to the Lord.

The pathos of Israel's relationship with God runs right through the book of Hosea, reflecting the understanding of God that Hosea gained from his personal experience of family and marriage. It is a mixture of love and grace, justice and forgiveness and tenderness and suffering. The complexity of the nature of God and his dealings with his covenant people presents a unique revelation that Hosea contributed to the eighth century revelation of God revealed through the Hebrew prophets.

1 HOSEA'S MARRIAGE   Hosea 1:1-11

The word of the Lord that came to Hosea son of Beeri during the reigns of Uzziah, Jotham, Ahaz and Hezekiah, kings of Judah, and during the reign of Jeroboam son of Joash king of Israel. When the Lord began to speak through Hosea, the Lord said to him, "Go, take to yourself an adulterous wife and children of unfaithfulness."

There are lots of problems with this opening statement, but it is important to get the historical background to the ministry of Hosea. As we said in the Introduction, the prophet Hosea was a resident of the northern kingdom of Israel with its capital at Samaria. We can date his ministry as immediately following that of Amos who also ministered in the northern kingdom about the middle of the eighth century BC. Jeroboam died in 752 BC and he is the only king of Israel mentioned here, so Hosea's ministry must have been in the closing years of his reign.

Jeroboam's 40-year reign had been a period of stability and economic growth that had caused the widespread sense of complacency which is what Amos had attacked so vigorously. Hosea is more concerned with the terrible sinfulness of the people of Israel breaking the covenant relationship with God which was like breaking a marriage covenant through adultery. He saw the whole land as being guilty of the vilest kind of adultery through the worship of other gods. It was to illustrate this spiritual adultery and what it meant to God that Hosea was instructed to go and marry a girl who was an adulterous wife.

We do not know why he selected Gomer, whether she was actively involved in prostitution or, as some biblical scholars believe, she was actually one of a team of girls serving men in one of the fertility cults that were up in the hills of Israel. Gomer soon conceived and bore a baby boy whom Hosea named 'Jezreel' which would have conveyed a message to the king and the political leaders in Samaria. Jezreel was the valley running from the foot of Mount Carmel east towards the Jordan River. It was renowned for its fertility and natural beauty. It was the place where Ahab had his summer residence and where

Elijah ran to seek shelter from the storm following the killing of Jezebel's priests.

Most significantly Jezreel was the place where Jehu slaughtered the whole house of Ahab including King Joram and Jezebel, Ahab's wife. By naming his son Jezreel, Hosea was obeying a word from the Lord saying that he would soon be punishing the house of Jehu for the massacre at Jezreel. This is somewhat strange because in 2 Kings 9, it is said that Yahweh had ordered Jehu to carry out his massacre, but here God promises to punish the house of Jehu for the massacre that they carried out at Jezreel. By calling his son Jezreel this was a sign that God was going to break the military might of Israel.

Gomer conceived again and she had a daughter whom Hosea was told to call *'Lo Ruhamah'*, meaning 'not loved' according to the footnote in most English Bibles; the Hebrew literally means 'compassion', rather than 'love'. The meaning here is that God will no longer show compassion upon the waywardness of the people of Israel who were worshipping other gods. They had the golden calf at Bethel, and they were told that he was the god who had brought them out of Egypt. This was a clear reference to the settlement in the land when the Canaanites told them that Baal was the owner who had to be worshipped if they were to enjoy fertility and produce food and water for their sustenance.

Verse 7 says that Judah will be spared the judgement that is going to fall upon Israel. The message for Israel is extremely hard and comes in the naming of the third child in Hosea's marriage. He was to be called *'Lo Ammi'* – 'Not Mine' – meaning that the people of Israel were no longer in a covenant relationship with God because they had turned to other gods.

This was a terrible indictment because God had actually chosen the family of Israel to be in a special relationship with him long before the covenant was established at Mount Sinai. In Exodus 3:7 God says, "*I have indeed seen the misery of my people in Egypt.*" He was already calling them "*my people*" and he made a promise to Moses, "*I will bring you out from under the yoke of the Egyptians . . . I will take you as my own people, and I will be your God*" (Ex 6:6-7).

Now, Hosea was saying the same as Amos had declared, that God would no longer protect a people who had deliberately broken the covenant by turning to other gods.

2 REUNION AND HOPE   Hosea 1:10 – 2:3

Yet the Israelites will be like the sand on the seashore, which cannot be measured or counted. In the place where it was said to them, "You are not my people" they will be called "sons of the living God".

This is a strange verse that completely reverses the previous verse which stated, *"You are not my people, and I am not your God."* It is worth noting at this stage that the Hebrew Bible, unlike all the English translations, finishes chapter 1 at verse 9. Chapter 2 begins at what we know as chapter 1:10 with this entirely new message reversing the previous verse and stating, "*In the place where it was said, 'you are not my people', they will be called 'sons of the living God'.*"

Biblical scholars have argued for many years about this passage of Scripture, with many concluding that this must be an editorial addition by those who did not like the finality of the judgement upon Israel of 1:9. Others have noted the historical situation that Hosea was facing shortly before the Assyrian invasion. The only way the words of Hosea could have survived is by being taken to Jerusalem where the scribes would have handled them to ensure that they were preserved for posterity. It is possible that at the time these words were being copied the Assyrian invasion had already taken place and there was hope during the reign of Josiah for a reunion with the northern kingdom of Israel which is reflected in the words of 1:10.

The same hope of reunion is found in Jeremiah and in Ezekiel. Jeremiah says, *"The days are coming, declares the Lord, when I will bring my people Israel and Judah back from captivity and restore them to the land I gave to their forefathers"* (Jer 30:3). Ezekiel was told to take two sticks of wood and write on one 'Judah' and the other 'Ephraim'. He was to join the two tightly together and he prophesied that the two nations would become one and would never again be divided (Ezek 37:15-22).

Some biblical scholars think that these later concepts of reunion became edited into the words of Hosea, to bring them into line with current expectations. It is, however, perfectly possible that Hosea saw the two outcomes, not as contradictory but as both being true within the purposes of God. He saw as clearly as Amos saw that God could no longer hold back the enemies of Israel when the whole nation had broken the covenant and turned to other gods. The holiness and the justice of God demanded that he should no longer protect this rebellious people.

Hosea, although fully in agreement with the words of Amos whom he was closely following, could see beyond the tragedy that was about to unfold whereby judgement would descend upon Samaria. He could see the longer-term purposes of God revealed to him, so he was able to say in adjoining verses, in the place where God said, *"you are not my people"* – they will be called, *"sons of the living God"* (1:10).

Hosea's major purpose was to reveal the nature of God that had been revealed to him through the agonies of heart that he suffered through his marriage to Gomer. He was privileged to glimpse the anguishes suffered by God through the waywardness of his people who deliberately turned their backs upon him and worshipped bits of wood and stone – turning away from the living God who loved them as a father loved a child.

Hosea foresaw the day when the different tribes of Israel would no longer emphasise their different identities, but they would recognise each other as brothers and sisters. They would *"say of your brothers, 'My people', and of your sisters, 'My loved one'."* (2:1). He could see the day of joyous reunion and even beyond that day when men and women would no longer even know which tribe they came from – they would be one people under God.

That is very largely the situation today, but it has taken over 3000 years of war, persecution and suffering. The Jewish people however have survived the centuries and are one people today with a common heritage but without the tribal distinctions. We should not put it beyond possibility that Hosea was looking far beyond the turmoil of his own day and the tragedy that he clearly foresaw happening to Israel.

The amazing thing that Hosea was foreseeing was the 'day of the Lord'. That day would be when his children would lose the negative prefix in each of their names – they would be *'Ruhamah'*, the one who is 'greatly loved', and *'Ammi'*, 'My people'. They would no longer be a divided people, but they would recognise each other as brothers and sisters – all belonging to God.

3 ISRAEL CALLED TO ACCOUNT   Hosea 2:2-17

Rebuke your mother, rebuke her for she is not my wife, and I am not her husband. Let her remove the adulterous look from her face and the unfaithfulness from between her breasts.

This section is a collection of poems with the intention of listing the adulterous practices of Israel running after false gods. It envisages a courtroom scene where the intention is to set out the charges of adultery. The objective, however, is not to lead to 'divorce' but to 'reconciliation'. It begins with a call to the children to undertake the rebuke of their mother because her husband is separated from her, but they are still her children.

The charge against the woman is that she attributes to Baal all the good things that she has enjoyed such as her food and water and all the produce of the land. The way of bringing her to understand the truth that it was God who supplied all these things is to turn her fertile land into thorn bushes and to put a wall around her so that she will be deprived of food and drink, and she will realise that she was better off with her husband. The outcome that God wanted to see was that she would acknowledge that it was God who gave her the grain, the new wine and oil, and who lavished all good things upon her. It was in order to get Israel to recognise that the prosperity they had enjoyed had not come from Baal, but from the God of Israel.

Therefore, God would take away his rain, his new wine, his wool and his linen so that she had nothing. All her religious festivals would be stopped. These celebrations were a mixture of pagan rites and Hebraic practices. They were the kind of syncretism that Jeremiah hated that used to be practised up in the hills outside Jerusalem and were even brought into the city where people erected altars on the roofs of their houses and at the street corners, which was why Jeremiah was told to stop praying for the welfare of the nation (Jer 7:16).

Verse 13 speaks of the terrible things that were happening in Israel in those days when they burned incense to the local gods and engaged in all their idolatrous practices, decking themselves with *"rings and jewellery"* and participating in the pagan rites of idolatry which included the fertility sex cults that were favourites among the men. This verse speaks of the punishment that God will bring upon the people of Israel, but it is strangely tempered in the next verse.

The wrath of God that is seen in the poems that outlined the faithlessness of the people of Israel and the punishment that their sins thoroughly deserved is followed in verse 14 with words that are exactly the same as those found in Isaiah 40:2 *"speak tenderly to Jerusalem"*. This brings an unexpected twist to the threat of judgement.

Hosea, through his own marriage to a promiscuous girl, was discovering something of immense significance which he brings into his understanding of God's reaction to the idolatrous behaviour of the people of Israel with whom God had formed a covenant relationship similar to that of marriage. He says in verse 14, *"Therefore I am now going to allure her; I will lead her into the desert and speak tenderly to her."*

This reference to the desert is to the early days when the people of Israel were brought out of slavery in Egypt and into the desert. It was there in the desert that they had to trust completely in God's provision of food and water. They had to get rid of their images of Egyptian gods that they had brought with them. It was there at the foot of Mount Sinai where the covenant relationship with God was established that they were told that the first commandment was that they should have no other God than Yahweh the God of Israel.

This 'desert experience' was intended to remind Israel of the days of their youth when they came out of Egypt. It would transform the *'valley of Achor'* into a *'door of hope'*. Achor was where Israel suffered a defeat in attempting to take the city of Ai. This was due to the disobedience of one man who had kept for himself booty that should have been devoted to God.

The 'door of hope' was that all Israel would totally renounce all practices of idolatry and that the name of Baal would never be heard again in the land. It would be banished from their lips. The life of the nation would be cleansed from idolatry and only the God of Israel worshipped among them. Hosea's message here is that God never stops longing for people to repent and return to him.

4 A NEW COVENANT RELATIONSHIP
Hosea 2:18-23

In that day I will make a covenant for them . . . I will betroth you to me you for ever.

'In that day' is a favourite phrase with the prophets indicating a day when God intervenes in the history of humanity to deal in righteousness and justice with his people. Here, Hosea is looking forward to a time when the people of Israel will no longer be enticed by the gods of the Canaanites with whom they had mixed the worship of Yahweh since the early days of the settlement in Canaan. It had been a widespread practice to call Yahweh by the name of Baal. This must be stopped for all time.

Hosea sees the day coming when God will make a fresh covenant for his people Israel. It will be a covenant reuniting his people with the world of nature – restoring the original harmony that existed before the fall of mankind. It is similar to the vision seen by Isaiah, *"The wolf will lie down with the lamb, the leopard will lie down with the goat . . ."* (Is 11:6-9). Isaiah's vision is set in the reign of the messianic kingdom. Hosea sees it as establishing a reign of peace in the world where the weapons of warfare are banished.

This will be the prelude to the new covenant relationship between God and his people, *"I will betroth you to me for ever."* This is the earliest mention among the prophets of a 'new covenant' – a relationship that is developed by Jeremiah (Jer 31:31). Hosea saw this new relationship in the setting of love and tenderness which was an entirely new concept in the religion of Israel.

Amos had emphasised the righteousness of the justice of God, but he had not grasped the concept of God actually loving his people tenderly; and he certainly had not reached the concept of the wrath of God as understood by Ezekiel in the Babylonian exile where he perceived God's righteous anger to be mixed in with a tender regard for the welfare of his people (Ezek 36:24-37).

The new scene that Hosea heard God promising was to reverse the estrangement with his people that had been caused by their unfaithfulness in worshipping Baal and other gods. He would establish a new relationship of love and trust in righteousness and justice with tender loving care and compassion. These were new sentiments in the relationship between God and the people of Israel. They were followed by a description of the blessings that would flow from the new relationship that would be established when Israel recognised the Sovereignty of God and was faithful to him.

Before we look at the blessings it is essential to understand the nature of the bond that God was to establish with his chosen people. It was very similar to the bond of 'remarriage' that Hosea was to enter into with Gomer, but it had not yet been recognised by Hosea himself. It was similar to the bond of betrothal.

The bond of betrothal was as sacred in Hebrew tradition as that of marriage with the one exception that it had not yet been consummated by physical intercourse. To be betrothed was to be in a two-way promise which demanded integrity and faithfulness. The promise of God was *"I will betroth you in righteousness and justice,"* also in love and compassion. All these elements were to be there at the heart of the new relationship between God and Israel – righteousness, justice, faithfulness, loyalty, integrity and love. This is a description of the bond between God and his people. They were the characteristics of the relationship that were both a promise from God and the nature of the response required from the people towards God.

The promises of God include ensuring that the earth will produce food for the people – grain, new wine and oil – the essentials for the sustenance of life. The blessings of God in the new relationship of righteousness and justice that God was promising for his people would reverse the disasters that had been foreseen that would result from unfaithfulness and idolatry. This reversal would change the names that had been given to Hosea's three children. The negative names would become positive, in the same way as the relationship between God and his people become transformed.

Jezreel would no longer be a scene of disaster, but a place of fertility and natural beauty. It would be a planting of the Lord like the Garden of Eden. The negative prefix of Hosea's children would be removed. The '*not loved*' child would become the loved one, and the '*not my people*' would now, in the new relationship with God, become his people. The people themselves would say, *"You are my God."*

5 THE REDEMPTION OF GOMER   Hosea 3:1-5

The Lord said to me, "Go, show your love to your wife again, though she is loved by another and is an adulteress. Love her as the Lord loves the Israelites, though they turn to other gods."

This little chapter of five verses looks quite straightforward as following on from chapter 1 but there are lots of difficulties. Hosea is told to go and show love to his wife again, but we have not been told that he ever stopped loving his wife and there was no suggestion in chapter 1 that Gomer left her husband after the birth of her third child whom Hosea had insisted on calling 'Not Mine', which could not have been easy for Gomer.

If we accept what some biblical scholars believe that this is another woman, we face even more difficulties because, quite clearly, Hosea is told to go and show love to his wife **again.** This would not be appropriate if it was a different woman. There are, however, real difficulties in knowing what had happened to Gomer. Did she go off with another man? Or, if she was originally one of the beautiful girls in a cultic harem serving the priests in their religious activities – is it possible that she had returned there? If this were the case it would account for Hosea having to purchase her freedom. This does not seem probable, however, because she is said to be loved by another man and she was in an adulterous relationship.

The price paid by Hosea for Gomer's freedom is a mystery. 15 shekels of silver was the standard rate at that time for purchasing a slave girl, but 'a homer' was a full donkey-load of grain. It is strange that the price paid for Gomer's freedom should be in two parts, one of which would require having a barn for its storage.

Hosea was told that he had to show love to his wife in the same way as God loved the Israelites who were an adulterous people turning to other gods and being addicted to sacred raisin cakes. This was a clear reference to Canaanite practices which had been a temptation to the Israelites since the settlement in Canaan. The raisin cakes were simply pressed grapes, but they were a special delicacy at the autumn harvest festival celebrations. Although they were Canaanite religious symbols they would also have been eaten at the feast of Tabernacles where they became one of the many syncretic practices that became incorporated into the religious life of the people of Israel.

Having purchased Gomer's freedom from whatever relationship she was in, Hosea made the condition that she was not to be involved in any sexual activities which included her relationship with him for an unspecified period of 'many days'. The instruction from God was that Hosea should *"love her as the Lord loves the Israelites, though they turn to other gods."*

This instruction is of great significance in the spiritual development of Hosea's life and ministry. It builds upon the original instruction to go and take a wife from an adulterous background. There was no mention of love at that stage, it was simply a transaction that Hosea had to make. This is the first mention of love and it may be that when he no longer had Gomer's company in his home, Hosea was eager to have her back. He really missed her and valued her.

Clearly, it was God's intention that Hosea should actually fall in love with Gomer so that he felt the pain of her defection and her relationship with another man. Through this experience Hosea began to glimpse the pain that God was experiencing through the defection of the people of Israel with whom he had entered a marriage covenant at Sinai and yet they had adopted other gods.

Hosea was the first prophet to get beyond the legal contract of Sinai in the giving of the law, which gave a severe view of God as, *"A jealous God, punishing the children for the sins of the fathers to the third and fourth generation of those who hate me, but showing love to a thousand generations of those who love me and keep my commandments"* (Deut 5:9-10).

It would be difficult to get an understanding of the immense, all-embracing and everlasting love of God from this statement. The pain and anxiety that Hosea experienced through Gomer's relationship with another man was beyond description. He was shown that the nation would go into exile where they would have no king or place of worship, but this would generate a desire among the people of Israel to seek the Lord and to come trembling before God seeking his forgiveness and to be embraced by his love.

6 THE CHARGE AGAINST ISRAEL   Hosea 4:1-13

Hear the word of the Lord, you Israelites, because the Lord has a charge to bring against you who live in the land: "There is no faithfulness, no love, no acknowledgement of God in the land."

This is the beginning of the main theme of Hosea's prophecies which runs right to the end of the book. This section sets out the case against the people of Israel in the form of a legal dispute which has its basis in the giving of the Decalogue at Mount Sinai. The people of Israel had broken the covenant by their faithlessness and their lack of understanding of God. Verse 2 sets out five charges of the nation breaking the commandments – swearing, lying, murdering, stealing, and committing adultery. As if this were not sufficient, it adds, *"bloodshed follows bloodshed"*. The consequence of this is the whole land is suffering as in a time of famine when everyone suffers from a lack of food and water.

Verse 4 is extremely difficult to translate due to the form of the Hebrew and this is why there are so many different translations in the different versions of the Bible. The final statement in the NIV, *"so I will destroy your mother"* appears in most versions, but it seems totally unconnected with the rest of the text. Some scholars have noted that the Hebrew word for 'mother' could be read as 'nation' which some versions such as the REB use, which certainly makes more sense.

The main charges are against the priests, not against the institution of the priesthood, but against priests who do not teach the people the truth about God. The central charge is *"my people are destroyed from lack of knowledge"* which is very similar to the charge against the priests brought by Jeremiah who found that the ordinary people did not know the requirements of God, so he went to the leaders, but they too *"had broken off the yoke"* (Jer 5:5). Jeremiah would almost certainly have read Hosea. More than a hundred years later he accused the priests of mishandling the word of God: *"The lying pen of the scribes has handled it falsely"* (Jer 8:8).

Hosea's charge that the people had no knowledge of God was because the priests had rejected truth, ignoring the Torah, the teaching of God. Both the priests and the prophets were guilty of not teaching the people the word of God. This also is very similar to charges that Jeremiah brought: *"The prophets prophesy lies, the priests rule by their own authority, but my people love it this way"* (Jer 5:31). Hosea says that because the priests and prophets had ignored the Torah, God also will ignore their children.

Hosea then brings a specific charge of the priests not only neglecting their duty to teach the word of God but they actually grew fat on the product of their sins. The specific charge was that they turned a blind eye to the sins of the people because the more people sinned the more sin offerings they brought to the altar. The priests themselves had charge of the sin offerings and it was their privilege to have a portion of each offering, so they benefited from the sins of the people. They actually relished the wickedness of the people from which they derived their food.

The charge against the priests did not end there, for many of them were deserting Yahweh and enjoying the fertility cults of the Canaanites and actually engaging in ritual prostitution. *"They sacrifice on the mountain tops and burn offerings on the hills."* The punishment for this would be severe and their young people would suffer from the sinfulness of their parents. The whole nation would come under judgement.

The reference to old wine and new that *"take away the understanding of my people"* could be referring to parties or to religious ceremonies at the mountaintop shrines that were obviously popular with the people of Israel and had been a great temptation to them ever since they moved in among the Canaanites. Hosea then uses biting sarcasm to refer to the ridiculous practice of worshipping a stick of wood and being so stupid as to think that they will get an answer to their prayers from a wooden idol.

The whole thrust of this piece is that the people do not know the God of Israel – the God who gave the commandments and established the covenant with his people in the time of Moses. This was the reason for their faithlessness – they simply did not know the truth. The covenant meant nothing to them, and this was the reason why they were running after wood and stone, the consequences of which would be disastrous for the nation.

7 THE DANGERS OF IDOLATRY   Hosea 4:14-19

I will not punish your daughters when they turn to prostitution, nor your daughters-in-law when they commit adultery, because the men themselves consort with harlots and sacrifice with shrine prostitutes.

This section continues the theme of chapter 4 where the central charge that Hosea brings against the people of Israel is that they lack knowledge of God because they have not been taught by the priests. The last verse of the previous section brought the charge that there was widespread idolatry. Men were going up into the mountain shrines and taking offerings to altars set up under oak trees or other places of prayer that were scattered around the countryside of the hill country of Israel.

This section begins with the threat of punishment to those engaged in this kind of ritual prostitution. But it was not the girls who were the focus of judgement in Hosea's eyes. His attention was directed towards the men among whom he discerned a spirit of harlotry. The very fact that the men encouraged their daughters and daughters-in-law to engage in shrine prostitution was a direct infringement of the law of God. In the teaching given by Moses, one of the declarations was, *"No Israelite man or woman is to become a shrine prostitute"* (Deut 23:17). So this form of harlotry was directly breaking the law of Israel.

Hosea recognised that the girls could not be held responsible for their sinful actions because they had no authority to offer their services at the Canaanites shrines without the permission of their fathers. Therefore, it was the men who were held responsible. They were the ones who were actively enjoying the services provided by the Canaanites' shrines.

Verse 15 presents a lot of difficulties because it is not only addressed to Israel but also to Judah. Hosea, himself a northerner, was ministering in Israel so there is no obvious reason why he should mention Judah. This has caused some scholars to conclude that this is an editorial note that was inserted later when Hosea's work was copied in Jerusalem after the destruction of Samaria. But Hosea clearly had a concern for all the people of Israel including Judah. In Jeremiah's day men from Judah were still using the fertility cults in Israel.

The second part of the verse says, *"Do not go to Gilgal, do not go up to Beth Aven"* – 'house of wickedness' – which was a prophetic reference to Bethel. This clearly is addressed to the northern kingdom as no one from Judah would consider going up to Bethel, but the warning here is against swearing an oath in the name of Yahweh the God of Israel at any of these high places of idolatry. To invoke the name of the Lord alongside pagan gods would be a terrible sin, and this warning was addressed to all the people of Israel.

Hosea then speaks of the stubbornness of Israel and the tenderness of God who longs to treat them like a good shepherd, caring for their needs as a shepherd cares for his lambs. This is specifically addressed to the people of Ephraim who were the ruling tribe of Israel – Jeroboam was from Ephraim. The statement *"Ephraim is joined to idols"* is a powerful indictment. It meant that they had actually become married to idolatry – they were conjoined and there was really nothing that could be done to separate them.

Verse 18 speaks of drinks and prostitution. It paints a vivid picture of the leaders involved in drunkenness and sexual corruption. Isaiah was ministering in Judah at about the same time. He also speaks of similar corruption, describing scenes of drunken orgies. He says, *"Priests and prophets stagger from beer and are befuddled with wine . . . All the tables are covered in vomit and there is not a spot without filth"* (Is 28:7-8). Clearly there was a great deal of corruption among the leaders of the nation, both in Judah and Israel.

Hosea says that their rulers love *"shameful ways"*. The Hebrew here for 'rulers' is *magen* which literally means 'a shield' – those who were to shield the nation from danger or harm. Clearly this was not what the leaders of the nation were doing. Both Hosea and Isaiah were proclaiming the same message, that those who should have been guarding the nation were guilty of leading them astray.

Judgement was inevitable. Hosea says, *"a whirlwind will sweep them away."* The powerful wind described here (Hebrew *ruach)* is the same word as is used in Ezekiel's vision of the valley of dry bones where he was commanded to prophesy to the breath of God, *"Come from the four winds, O breath, and breathe into these slain that they may live"* (Ezek 37:9). The breath of God would cause them to be ashamed of their idolatry.

8 INEVITABILITY OF JUDGEMENT   Hosea 5:1-7

Hear this, you priests! Pay attention, you Israelites! Listen, O royal house! This judgement is against you. You have been a snare at Mizpah, a net spread out on Tabor.

Hosea had given warnings of judgement in chapter 4. Here he strengthens the warnings to direct commands. People, priests and the Royal household including the political leaders of the nation, are commanded to listen because there is a pronouncement of judgement against them. Collectively they have acted in a way that has trapped the nation, like spreading snares or nets for catching birds. The leaders, priests and politicians, are deeply involved in misleading the nation and they will now have to pay the price of their rebellion against God.

God had been watching what was happening in Ephraim. There is a similar pronouncement at the end of Jeremiah's 'Temple Sermon' where he says, *"But I have been watching! Declares the Lord"* (Jer 7:11). Similarly, here God says that he has been observing what was happening in Israel and the way the people had turned to prostitution, which in this case means that there was widespread use of the Canaanites' fertility cult shrines.

Verse 4 says that their deeds do not permit them to return to their God. They were so heavily involved in idolatry that it had virtually taken control of their minds. They were obsessed by a 'spirit of prostitution' as men today become obsessed with pornography. An evil spirit controls their lives. They no longer even acknowledged the God of Israel. For a long time, since the early days of the settlement in Canaan, the Israelites had practised a form of syncretism whereby they paid homage to the local Baal who was thought to be owner of the land and therefore controlled its fertility, but they also continued to acknowledge Yahweh the God of Israel.

What Hosea was saying was that idolatry in the form practised by the sex cults had so taken hold of the people of Israel that they were actually possessed by a 'spirit of prostitution'. Israel no longer acknowledged their God and for many people in Judah this was the same situation.

This situation for both nations was so serious that at the festivals when they go seeking the Lord they will not find him. This is a reference to the widespread practice of the pagan religions surrounding Israel whereby their god disappears or dies at a particular season. The worshippers then go seeking him and they have to carry out particular rituals in order to resurrect him. If they did not know the right forms of worship which were often secret practices known only to the initiated, they would not find their deity.

It was this ritual that Ezekiel discovered was actually being practised in the temple in Jerusalem in one of his ecstatic visits before the glory of the Lord departed. Ezekiel was being taken on a conducted tour of the temple when he was taken to the North gate where, to his horror, he *"saw women sitting there, mourning for Tammuz"* (Ezek 8:14). They were practising the rituals required for calling back Tammuz who they were no doubt hoping would help them during the Babylonian siege of Jerusalem.

Hosea's reaction to the depths of idolatry into which the people of Israel had sunk was to declare that when the people took their flocks for sacrifices to the Lord, they would not find him. There would be no special rituals or prayers that they could offer to bring him back. The God of Israel had withdrawn from the land because of the unfaithfulness of the people.

There was no excuse for the leaders of the nation, as Hosea had said, there was 'no acknowledgement of God'. He had narrowed this charge to the priests who had failed to teach the people the truth of the word of God. Both priests and prophets had stumbled into sin. They had failed to teach the people, so, he said, *"My people are destroyed from lack of knowledge"* (Hosea 4:6).

The inevitable judgement of breaking the covenant was clearly set out in the Law, *"If you reject my decrees and abhor my laws and fail to carry out all my commands and so violate my covenant, then I will do this to you: I will bring upon you sudden terror, wasting diseases and fever . . ."* (Lev 26:14-19). Similarly in Deuteronomy 28 from verse 15, warnings of the curses that would follow disobedience were clearly set out. The Torah was given to enable the people to know the requirements of the Lord, but the priests and the leaders had failed to teach the people, so the whole nation had gone astray and they and the land would suffer the terrible judgement of destruction that was coming upon Israel.

9 BATTLE STATIONS   Hosea 5:8-15

Sound the trumpet in Gibeah, the horn in Ramah. Raise the battle cry in Beth Aven, lead on, O Benjamin. Ephraim will be laid waste on the day of reckoning. Among the tribes of Israel I proclaim what is certain.

This passage in Hosea recounts events in both Israel and Judah during an unstable period in their history. Hosea was told to sound the trumpet of warning in three towns in the south of Israel along the borders with Judah – Gibeah, Ramah, and Beth Aven – the 'house of wickedness' which may have been a nickname for Bethel. Strong warnings were given by Hosea acting as watchman to both Israel and Judah where relationships between the two had usually been tense ever since the days of Jeroboam I and Rehoboam.

Judah's leaders are said here to be untrustworthy and doing things like those who move boundary stones. Judah had evidently taken advantage of the unsettled political situation in Israel and annexed some of Israel's territory. This was regarded as a particularly deceitful thing to do, to steal a neighbour's territory by moving the boundary stones which was roundly condemned in Deuteronomy 19:14.

Another particularly wicked thing that Judah had done in the eyes of Israel was to appeal for help from the king of Assyria. Hosea says that it was Israel who turned to Assyria for help, but 2 Kings 16:7 says, *"Ahaz sent messengers to say to Tiglath-Pileser king of Assyria I am your servant and vassal come up and save me out of the hand of the king of Aram and of the king of Israel."* Although it may be that what Hosea is referring to here is Menahem's bribing Tiglath-Pileser, recounted in 2 Kings 15:19. All the most wealthy men in Israel were forced to give 50 shekels of silver to the king of Assyria.

The background here is the unstable period in Israel that followed the death of Jeroboam II. His son Zechariah only lasted a few months before he was assassinated and there followed two other kings in quick succession. On the international scene Tiglath-Pileser had succeeded to the throne in Assyria in 745 BC and he was keen to expand his empire westward towards the Mediterranean Sea.

This placed Syria and Israel under threat and the two states who were usually enemies entered into a treaty of alliance which they asked Judah to join. Ahaz, who had only just succeeded his father Jotham, refused to join them. Consequently, a combined army of Israel and Syria attacked Jerusalem. It was at this stage that Ahaz appealed to Assyria for help and there was a willing response. Assyria attacked Damascus and annexed Syria as well as some of the Northern Territory of Israel.

Ahaz went to Damascus to meet Tiglath-Pileser where he saw an altar for one of the gods of Assyria which he copied and had erected in the temple in Jerusalem on which he offered the morning and evening sacrifice according to 2 Kings 16. All this is the historical background to the warnings that Hosea was bringing to both Israel and Judah. Both their leaders were ungodly men leading their people astray. Hosea was bringing strong warnings of disaster that lay ahead for both nations. He could see that Assyria would not bring peace and security to Judah but trusting the Assyrians would lead to judgement upon both nations.

A central message of all the Hebrew prophets was trust in God. It was part of the conditions of the covenant that the people of Israel should have no other deity and they should be absolutely loyal and faithful to Yahweh. For this reason, the prophets were generally against any alliances with other nations because this usually entailed recognition of their gods. This was part of the price that Ahaz paid for peace between Judah and Assyria.

Hosea sees that what is happening in Ephraim is like a moth that quietly eats away cloth if undisturbed and he uses a similar metaphor for Judah where he sees corruption like dry rot slowly destroying the nation. Both nations were heading for disaster because they did not put their trust totally and solely in the God of their fathers. God will be like a lion attacking both Israel and Judah.

Verse 14 foresees Assyria carrying into exile the people of Israel after the fall of Samaria. He speaks of the nation being torn to pieces with no one to rescue them because God will not protect them. God will be hidden from them until they admit their guilt and repent, seeking the face of God in their misery.

10 UNREPENTANT ISRAEL   Hosea 6:1-8

"Come, let us return to the Lord. He has torn us to pieces, but he will heal us; he has injured us but he will bind up our wounds. After two days he will revive us: on the third day he will restore us, that we may live in his presence."

This word from Hosea at the start of chapter 6 appears to be a response to the harsh threat in 5:14 and 15. This strong threat of judgement was because the sins of Israel and Judah were driving Yahweh to leave the nation to their fate. They would not see his presence again until they earnestly sought him. But here Hosea may just be citing a false piety which now assumed that God would reverse everything and bless them, healing wounds he had inflicted. Because, *"After two days he will revive us . . ."* has nothing to do with national spiritual resurrection. It referred to the pagan nature deities who were said to die and rise again after a few days of festivities. The people were confusing these pagan rites with the God of Israel.

The assumption here is that all they have to do is to turn to God and cry out to him in their misery and he will immediately respond restoring the people to a state of blessing. They were confident that God would respond immediately. He was totally reliable – as surely as the sun rises, he would respond to their cries and, like the spring rains he would bring an abundance of blessing upon his people.

All this means that the people had not repented at all. All they had done was to express regrets about their misery and cry out to God. That was not repentance! *"O Ephraim what shall I do with you?"* This expresses God's love, anger, and frustration just as a loving parent sometimes feels towards a naughty child. What can he do with Ephraim and Judah? Their love was like the morning mist that evaporates because there is no substance in it.

God had sent them warnings and judgements, interpreted by prophets as in Amos 4, *"Many times I struck your gardens and vineyards, I struck them with blight and mildew; but you have not returned to me, declares the Lord"* (Am 4:9). God's judgements had flashed like lightning upon them, but they had simply been ignored.

What was lacking in both Israel and Judah was any sense of remorse. The opening phrase in chapter 6 is, *"Come, let us return to the Lord."* It was as though all they had to do was to turn around and acknowledge Yahweh as their God and all would be well. He would reverse their misfortunes and shower them with blessings. They simply had to try harder or shout louder and then God would respond.

Clearly, this was a case whereby they did not know the God of their fathers. Hosea had already complained bitterly that the priests had not done their job in teaching what God had given them through Moses, so the people did not know their God. This is why there was no substance in their turning to God.

They recognised that something was wrong. They could not ignore the hardships that they were enduring, but although the signs that God had sent were rightly interpreted to them by the prophets, they had not responded in repentance. Hosea does not identify the prophets, but we know that he followed both Amos in Samaria and Isaiah in Jerusalem, both of whom had faithfully declared the word of the Lord.

It would appear from verse 9 that the words of the prophets had been discarded, and not even understood. Hence the word Hosea brought was, *"I desire mercy, not sacrifice."* The word 'mercy' here (Hebrew *chesed*) is better translated as 'loving-kindness'). People had responded with sacrifices and burnt offerings, but that was not what God was looking for. He wanted evidence of their love for him and their loyalty and faithfulness to him. This required a total change of mindset and remorse for their unfaithfulness. What God wanted to see in his people was a relationship of love and trust.

The people were just like Adam, the archetypal sinner, who broke his relationship with God. They too were unfaithful and wicked, staining the very ground with the blood of the innocent. How could God use such a depraved and corrupt people as *'his own'* people through whom he would reveal his nature and purposes to the nations? Gilead is singled out as an example. Gilead was one of the cities of refuge and therefore should have been a city where the covenant obligations were upheld and whose citizens were renowned for their righteousness, but it was quite the reverse, it was full of wickedness, of injustice and bloodshed.

11 IMMEDIATE RESTORATION IMPOSSIBLE
Hosea 6:9 – 7:7

As marauders lie in ambush for a man, so do bands of priests, they murder on the road to Shechem, committing shameful crimes. I have seen a horrible thing in the house of Israel. There Ephraim is given to prostitution and Israel is defiled.

This is not an easy passage to interpret because we cannot be sure of what Hosea is referring to about murder on the road to Shechem. The best explanation is that the incident that Hosea has in mind is the one described in Judges 9 where the 70 sons of Gideon were murdered at Shechem by Abimelech. It was an infamous incident in the history of Israel that brought shame upon the nation. It was all mixed in with worship at the Canaanite shrine and here Hosea may be referring to priests of Baal rather than priests of Yahweh.

Hosea sees the same kind of spiritual prostitution defiling the nation in his day as happened back in the time of the Judges. Both Israel and Judah were defiled by idolatry to such an extent that even basic law and order had now broken down among the people of Samaria. People broke into one another's houses and there were bands of robbers, so that it was not safe to walk on the streets.

These were conditions that existed in Israel in the years following the death of Jeroboam II when his son Zachariah inherited the throne. He was assassinated by Shallum who himself was murdered by Menahem who lasted 10 years, and he was succeeded by Pekahiah before he also was assassinated. It was a highly unstable period, not only in the leadership of the nation but at every level of society.

Hosea speaks of God's desire to heal the nation. He was speaking about all the Lord's people, both Israel and Judah. Whenever God intended forgiving them the crimes of Israel were so terrible that they could not be ignored. This is reflecting the sentiment expressed in 6:6, where God expressed his desire to see lovingkindness among his people rather than lots of religious sacrifices.

Hosea has reached the central theme of his message, and he returns to it here, seeing the impossibility of God forgiving the nation when their crimes were so blatant. This was a terrible period in the history of the people of Israel. Their personal relationships with one another were characterised by deceitfulness and the whole nation was engulfed in lawlessness so they had no regard for the fact that God could see what was happening – that clearly was of no value to them.

It was not just the ordinary people who were involved in sinful practices, but kings and princes were renowned for their lives of intrigue and deceitfulness. This reference to kings and princes is ambiguous, but it clearly reflects the turbulent period in the leadership of the nation. It is followed by the statement, *"They are all adulterers, burning like an oven."*

It is never easy when any of the prophets speak of adultery to know whether they are referring to idolatry or to personal morality. In this case it could be either, or even both, because the whole nation was in such a turbulent time. The leaders in Samaria were engaged in conspiracies and plots to carry out murder that involved violent groups among the rich and powerful families. These were the people whom Amos had particularly targeted with his powerful warnings of what would happen to them.

Hosea picked up this theme, but he brought a theological perspective on all the intrigue and deceitful practices. He saw the impossibility of God's forgiveness. In verse 5 Hosea referred to the coronation of a new king. We cannot be sure which one is referred to here, but it is most likely to be King Hoshea who was appointed by the Assyrians in 731 BC.

Hoshea was initially supportive of Assyria, and he brought a measure of peace and security to Israel. Sadly, he listened to the advice of the pro-Egyptian group of advisers to the monarchy and he made a secret deal with Egypt which evidently became known to the Assyrians. They promptly sent their army who carried out a widespread attack upon villages and towns right across Israel. They also laid siege to Samaria which lasted for three years and caused enormous suffering to the people in the city. They also carried out a mass population transfer – deporting whole towns and communities to other parts of the Assyrian Empire and bringing in foreigners to settle in the Israeli towns, thus destroying the ancient heritage of Israel. The tragedy of these days is summed up in 2 Kings 17:13-14, *"The Lord warned Israel and Judah through all his prophets . . . but they would not listen."*

12 ALLIANCES WITH FOREIGN NATIONS
Hosea 7:8-16

Ephraim mixes with the nations; Ephraim is a flat cake not turned over. Foreigners sap his strength, but he does not realise it. His hair is sprinkled with grey, but he does not notice. Israel's arrogance testifies against him.

This is one of the most important passages in the Bible for giving us a glimpse of the nature of God – the God of Israel, the God of Abraham, Isaac and Jacob, the God and Father of our Lord Jesus Christ. It begins with continuing the metaphor of 'an oven' started in the first half of chapter 7 where the focus was upon the heat of the fire. The emphasis here is upon the cake that has not been properly cooked – which makes it not fit for purpose. It is inedible; it is half-baked, and useless.

The metaphor is about Israel. The people are so stupid and arrogant that they are totally unaware of the reality of their own condition. They are doing everything in their own strength, relying upon their own maturity – grey hair that should bring the wisdom of age is totally missing. They are as stupid as a bird flying from one perch to another with no discernible purpose and can easily be trapped.

This is what they have done in their international politics, rushing from one half-baked alliance to another, making an alliance with Syria, and then turning to Assyria and forming an alliance, and then breaking their agreement with them and turning to Egypt. The folly of this political turntable is almost unbelievable! It will inevitably lead to disaster. *"Woe to them, because they have strayed from me! Destruction to them, because they have rebelled against me!"*

Hosea sees all this as rebellion against God. It is immediately followed by words that are wet with tears of grief that fall from the eyes of God. *"I long to redeem them."* Redemption is costly – there was a price to pay to redeem someone who had been captured by an enemy, but God was willing to pay any price to redeem his beloved ones – if only they would trust him.

They cry out to God for blessings and prosperity, for grain, for wine, but they do not put their trust in the Lord. They turn away from him to others, to nations that worship false gods and have no respect for the God of Israel. They even turned to Egypt who made a laughingstock of them, scorning their advances.

The grief in the heart of God was that the people of Israel with whom he entered into a covenant relationship of love and trust had gone so far from him in making these alliances with other nations. This was a form of idolatry and rebellion against the Lord, the God of Israel. Even their prayers and their worship did not come from a pure heart. It was more like wailing upon their beds. They were just like children crying out for food and drink and anything they wanted.

It is at this point that the grief of God revealed through the ministry of Hosea is unique. He is **the first** of the prophets of Israel to recognise the level of suffering in the heart of God through the waywardness of his people Israel with whom he had made a covenant of love and trust. It was God who had trained them and strengthened them, but they still did not trust him. They turned away from their own God – the Lord Most High, the One and only God of Creation. Their faith was like 'a faulty bow' that had lost its strength and was useless in the time that it was needed.

The reference to gathering together for grain and new wine is probably a reference to the coronation celebrations of each of the succession of kings who came to the throne through the shedding of blood. *"The leaders will fall by the sword"* is a clear reference to what had happened since the death of Jeroboam II with the murder of one king after another and the turmoil that spread right through the nation from the leadership.

All this revealed the sinful state of the nation that was the inevitable result of the consistent unfaithfulness of the people of Israel in turning away from God. The summary in 2 Kings 17:14-20, emphasises the magnitude of the sinfulness of the people in deserting their God – *"They rejected his decrees and the covenant he had made with their fathers and the warnings he had given them"* (2 Kgs 17:15). The central part of this passage is the grief in the heart of God that is revealed by Hosea in the words, *"They have strayed from me"* . . . *"I long to redeem them"* . . . *"They do not cry out to me with their hearts."*

13 REAPING THE WHIRLWIND   Hosea 8:1-10

Put the trumpet to your lips! An eagle[2] is over the house of the Lord because the people have broken my covenant and rebelled against my law.

There are a number of significant points in this passage that help us to understand the new perspective that Hosea brings among the Eighth Century prophets. It begins with the command to put the trumpet to the lips. This command is in the singular in the Hebrew, so it is usually thought that it is a personal command to Hosea. The Eagle over the house of the Lord is clearly Assyria and the reference here is to Bethel and the general context indicates that this was said in the time of King Hoshea who had made a pact with Assyria.

The statement *"The people have broken my covenant and rebelled against my law"* (teaching), is very significant. Hosea is the only one of the eighth century prophets to speak about the covenant. They all speak of the Torah and refer to parts of the Pentateuch, but apart from one doubtful reference in Isaiah 33:8, no other eighth century BC prophet focuses upon the covenant.

Hosea's perspective is different from the others in that period. 'Covenant' is all to do with relationships. It is similar to a marriage covenant that binds a man and a woman together in an intimate relationship of love, faithfulness and trust that should last for ever. This was the nature of the covenant that was established and mutually agreed at Sinai. Clear terms were set out and agreed by both parties- God and the people of Israel – from henceforward he would be their God, and they would be his people.

God and Israel were bound together in a marriage relationship of love and trust. This kind of relationship was what the whole of Hosea's ministry centred upon, and this was why his marriage was so important. It was a sacred covenant binding husband and wife together in a relationship of love and mutual trust, forsaking all others. Israel and God were bound together in a similar binding relationship.

Israel had broken the covenant and rebelled against the teaching that was an integral part of the covenant. Nevertheless, they still

---

2 *"A vulture"* is actually a better translation.

cried out to God that they acknowledged him. But what did that acknowledgement mean because they had rejected what was good? They had not only set up their own king when they broke away from the house of Judah, but they were setting up more kings and princes in these turbulent years of their history without even consulting the Lord. Hosea was ministering at a time when there had been a succession of kings who had met violent ends, none of whom had been appointed by God.

Back in the early days of the settlement, the people of Israel had asked Samuel for a king because they wanted to be like all the other nations (1 Sam 8). Now, they had done something even more sinful in paying silver and gold to the king of Assyria with whom they had entered a covenantal agreement whereby he would protect them. They had actually put their trust in a man who served pagan gods. This would contaminate the land of Israel that belonged to Yahweh, the God of Israel. This was a direct rebellion against God.

Although Hosea centred his teaching upon the love of God, he also knew God to be a God of justice, and the outrageous behaviour of Israel incurred the righteous anger of God which he knew would bring inevitable judgement. This led to the direct command, *"Throw out your calf idol Samaria! My anger burns against them. How long will they be incapable of purity?"* This is probably the hardest word uttered in Hosea's ministry.

The golden calf at Bethel had been put there in 922 BC by Jeroboam I who had deceived Israel that this was their God who had brought them up out of Egypt – but it had been made in Israel by craftsmen: it was not God! The calf of Samaria would be broken in pieces. The people of Israel had sown the wind and now they would reap the whirlwind. Nothing good would happen. They would not even enjoy good harvests. Even if they did grow grain, it would be enjoyed by foreigners, because they were going to be swallowed up by the nations.

In putting their trust in Assyria, they had sold themselves to pagans. They were like a wild donkey wandering around, not knowing where to go and having no master, and no secure home. The people of Israel had sold themselves to foreigners and this would bring inevitable judgement. The nation of Israel was destined to waste away under the oppression of the pagan king in whom they had put their trust.

14 THE DESTINY OF ISRAEL AND JUDAH
Hosea 8:11-14

Though Ephraim built many altars for sin offerings, these have become altars for sinning. I wrote for them the many things in my law, but they regarded them as something alien.

These verses begin with a direct word from God. They bring a charge that goes back to the reign of Jeroboam I who revolted against Rehoboam and established the kingdom of Israel. He did not want the people of Israel to go up to Jerusalem for the festivals which would have acknowledged the supremacy of Judah. Jeroboam therefore established two major sanctuaries, at Bethel and Dan. In each he placed an altar with a golden calf and told the people that this was the God of Israel who had brought them out of Egypt. This was a deception for which God would hold him responsible.

When Amos had seen a prayer picture of the Lord with a plumbline in his hand he received the word, *"The high places of Israel will be destroyed, and the sanctuaries of Israel will be ruined"* (Am 7:9). Hosea would have been well aware of this,

In addition to the two central shrines, altars for sacrificing offerings to Yahweh the God of Israel, were placed at a number of the Canaanites' shrines up in the hills of Israel so that local people did not have to make long journeys to Bethel or Dan but could make their offerings on altars alongside those of Baal. This led to forms of syncretism, the mixing of Baal and Yahweh, that was condemned by the prophets. These altars for the sin offerings of the people became 'altars of sinning'.

We know that the Levites refused to officiate at these places in Israel. As a consequence, Jeroboam appointed anyone who volunteered to be a priest, which, of course was shocking to the people of Judah. *"Jeroboam built shrines on the high places and appointed priests from all sorts of people, even though they were not Levites"* (1 Kgs 12:31). These priests evidently made their own rules, ignoring those written in the Torah regulating sin offerings which had to be handled by the Levites, from which priests were allocated a share of the meat. Hence, more sin in the nation meant more food on the priests' tables.

The priests took whatever meat they wanted for themselves before making the burnt offerings on the altars. This was displeasing to the Lord and he would be remembering their wickedness from which punishment would result.

All these malpractices came from the disregard of the law at Mount Sinai delivered to Israel through Moses. The wide range of rules and regulations set out in the Torah was given for the guidance of the people, to enable them to know the behaviour that was required of those who were in a covenant relationship with God. It was God himself who had written these rules, but the people of Israel had regarded them as 'something alien' – something that could be discarded as useless for them now that they were free from the restrictions imposed by the temple priests in Jerusalem.

The threat in verse 13 was that God's punishment was going to be to return the people of Israel to the condition they were in prior to the assembly at Mount Sinai. When they were in Egypt, they were not the people of God, bound to him by a covenant relationship. They were not really even a nation, but they were the family of Jacob enslaved by the Egyptians and suffering under the oppression of slavery.

It was God who had set them free – heeding their cries, and he had demanded their freedom from the Egyptians so that they could come out and worship him. He was the one who had saved them, but *"Israel had forgotten his maker."* Therefore, God was going to withdraw his presence, his protection and his blessings and leave the people to their own devices.

The people of Israel had built palaces (or temples) and built great fortified cities such as Samaria. Judah had done the same, fortifying a number of their cities and building up their defences against attack from enemies. Both Israel and Judah had built armed forces and Israel, in particular, was very proud of its army and boasted of its fortifications. Clearly, for both nations their trust was in the strength of their armies, not in God.

Both Israel and Judah had turned their backs upon God, not looking to him as their Maker and Redeemer who had saved them from Egypt. As a result of their wickedness God would remove his cover and allow enemies to come and destroy their fortifications. Their cities would be destroyed by fire and all their fortifications would be consumed.

15 THE FESTIVALS OF GOD   Hosea 9:1-9

Do not rejoice, O Israel; do not be jubilant like the other nations. For you have been unfaithful to your God; you love the wages of a prostitute at every threshing floor. Threshing floors and wine presses will not feed the people.

This whole section is about the feast of Tabernacles. Tabernacles was one of the three great feasts of Israel that were all connected with harvest. Exodus 23 from verse 14 says that all three feasts were celebration events which were sacred thanksgivings – times of worship, recognising the goodness of God who supplied the food for life.

The feast of unleavened bread was to be celebrated for seven days in Abib when no yeast was eaten, remembering the hurried exit from Egypt. Secondly, the feast of the first fruits of crops was to be held; and then at the end of the agricultural year the final harvest celebrated the in-gathering of the fruits of the vine, the olive tree, and the figs – giving thanks for wine, oil, and fruit. But this was not simply a community event with an opportunity to drink wine, sing and dance. It was a sacred occasion when all the people were required to come before God. *"Three times a year all the men are to appear before the Sovereign Lord"* (Ex 23:17).

Because it was a requirement for all men to go to the three celebration events, this meant a lot of travelling, especially for those who lived a long way from Jerusalem or Bethel. In order to lessen the burden of travelling, some of the old Canaanite shrines in the hills were opened for use especially at Tabernacles. Inevitably there was a mixing with the practices of Baal. This is what Hosea has in mind when he speaks about *"threshing floors and wine presses"* being used.

Tabernacles was known as 'the great feast': it was the most important event of the year, often known as 'booths' because the children of Israel were said to have lived in booths during the years they spent in the wilderness. *"Live in booths for seven days"* is the command in the law (Lev 23:42). Booths were temporary shelters consisting of four wooden rods covered with twigs and leaves, but we do not know how long the Israelites actually lived in booths, because most of the time on their travels through the wilderness for 40 years until they reached Canaan they were living in tents.

Tabernacles was always a time of great rejoicing, but Hosea says that they should not rejoice. It sounds as though he was actually at a celebration of Tabernacles, probably at Bethel or Dan, or even up in the hills at a popular shrine. His message certainly would not have been popular among the celebrants. He was bitterly critical of the people who he said were unfaithful to the God of Israel. They loved the sexual practices at the shrines and at the altars set up on threshing floors.

Hosea warned that the sinfulness of the people was such that God was going to return them to the same conditions they had been in when they were in Egypt before God rescued them. It would not be Egypt where they were going, but Assyria and there they would be forced to eat unclean food. They would not have the opportunity of offering sacrifices to the Lord when they were deported to a foreign land. They would not be able to celebrate at the festivals even if they survived the destruction that was coming upon the land. Hosea's message was *"the days of reckoning are at hand. Let Israel know this."*

Far from the message being received in penitence, it was greeted with great hostility. The statement in verse 7 that *"the prophet is considered a fool, the inspired man a maniac"* sounds as though Hosea is speaking from personal experience, and his message was dismissed. There can be no doubt that Hosea was dismayed. He perceived the role of the prophet to which he was called was to be a watchman for the nation.

This meant understanding the times in which he was living and acting as a lookout upon the city walls – blowing the trumpet of warning of danger. During the exile in Babylon Ezekiel developed this concept (Ezek 33). The reference to 'hostility in the house of God' is clearly the reaction to Hosea's denunciation of what was happening, but his final reference to Gibeah is unclear. Most biblical scholars believe it to be a reference to the terrible events recorded in Judges 19 – 21 of the rape and murder of a Levite's concubine, which was a reminder of the sinfulness of the people that was still there now, and there was no sign of repentance.

16 GRAPES IN THE DESERT   Hosea 9:10-17

When I found Israel, it was like finding grapes in the desert, when I saw your fathers, it was like seeing the early fruit on the fig-tree. But when they came to Baal Peor, they consecrated themselves to that shameful idol.

This is a piece that is based upon Hosea's understanding of the love of God for the people of Israel and his deep sadness at their failure to respond adequately to his love. It begins with a well-known oracle current at his time of the unexpected joy of finding grapes in the desert. Of course, grapes do not grow in the wilderness! So, it was a figure of speech expressing great pleasure that was totally unexpected.

Hosea recalls the history of Israel at Mount Sinai when the people of Israel whom God had just rescued from Egypt, gathered around Moses to listen to the word of the Lord. God was delighted to see those who were from different tribes with no national identity coming before him to recognise him as their God. It was a moment of great joy for God. When he saw the forefathers of Israel "*it was like seeing the early fruit on the fig tree.*"

The first fruits were always the tastiest. They were the first fruits of the harvest and the pleasure they gave was indescribable. God was expressing his overwhelming joy that the family of Abraham, Isaac and Jacob had at last come together after all their squabbling and suffering in the iron furnace of slavery in Egypt.

They had come before him, acknowledging him as the God of Israel and he had responded by establishing a covenant of peace with them through which he would be their God and they would be his people. At that time God had said, *"Now if you obey me fully and keep my commandments, then out of all the nations you will be my treasured possession . . . You will be for me a kingdom of priests and a holy nation"* (Ex 19:5-6).

This expression of the expectation of God that his people would fulfil his purpose of revealing himself to the world through them was at the heart of the Mount Sinai experience. God's disappointment is expressed in recounting two incidents in the early history of the people of Israel. The first was when they came to Baal Peor in an incident recorded in Numbers 25 where the men of Israel indulged in sexual immorality with Moabite women and joined in worshipping the Baal of Peor.

The consequences of this incident were a catastrophe for Israel through which many people died, but it was the cause of great grief to God because the Israelite men had actually 'yoked themselves' with the Baal of Peor. This was a direct betrayal of the God of Israel. Because of this shameful thing the presence of God – his glory – had left Israel; it flew away 'like a bird'.

The theme throughout this chapter had centred on the great feast of Tabernacles. All those who went to the feast went with two expectations – first, that the presence of the God of Israel would be there, and they could actually enter his presence. Second, that the blessings of fertility would be renewed. As they rejoiced over the reaping of the harvest at the end of the agricultural year so they would see the first rains coming to soften the soil preparing for the sowing of the seed that would ensure the fertility of the next season and provide for a future harvest.

Hosea's message hits at the very heart of this expectation. He says that when the glory of the Lord departs, all fertility will be taken away. There will be *"no birth, no pregnancy, no conception"*. Even if the women did manage to conceive, God would not allow them to bring up their children, they would be bereaved.

The second incident in Israel's history that grieved the Lord was what happened at Gilgal which Hosea says, caused God to hate them; but we have no idea what happened at Gilgal. There is nowhere in the history of Israel showing any atrocities that took place there. The nearest we get is a vague reference in Amos 4:4 where he says *"go to Gilgal and sin yet more"* which probably means that there was a high place there of Canaanite worship.

The sins of the people of Israel over the centuries had now reached the point where God says, *"I will drive him out of my house. I will no longer love them,"* and this is followed by Hosea's final statement, *"My God will reject them because they have not obeyed him."* The consequence of this is what is described in the Septuagint as the *'diaspora'* – the great dispersal of the people of Israel across the Gentile nations of the world.

17 THE CONSEQUENCES OF DISOBEDIENCE
Hosea 10:1-11

Israel was a spreading vine; he brought forth fruit for himself. As his fruit increased, he built more altars, as his land prospered, he adorned his sacred stones.

Chapter 10 completes the series of historical reflections upon the sins of Israel and the dire consequences of their unfaithfulness to God. Each of these has the underlying motive of establishing the justice of God in the calamities and judgements that fall upon the nation of Israel. The first two verses are strange because they are all written in the third person which poses the question, 'who is being addressed by Hosea?' There are no clues to provide an answer.

The opening statement is unclear. The KJV says, *"Israel is an empty vine"*, whereas the NRSV says the exact opposite, *"Israel is a luxuriant vine"*, while the NIV that we are following in this study compromises with, *"Israel was a spreading vine"*. The problem lies with the Hebrew *boqeq* that comes from the root *boqaq,* meaning to overflow. This is one of many problems that arise from the earliest Hebrew manuscripts not having vowels and uncertainty as to which vowels are intended, especially if we do not have the same word repeated in other parts of the Bible for comparison.

The blessings of the Lord upon the people of Israel had certainly overflowed, but this is not what is being conveyed here. Hosea probably had in mind Psalm 80 which speaks of God bringing a vine out of Egypt, driving out the nations and planting the vine which took root and filled the land (Ps 80:8-11). Hosea follows that statement by making it clear that Israel had used its prosperity for its own enrichment and the altars and sacred stones it had installed were not to honour God.

Verse 2 states the offence and the punishment that must follow. *"The heart is deceitful, and now they must bear their guilt."* Their altars and their sacred stones were going to be demolished by God. The people would complain that they did not have a king, The nation was in such a mess that false oaths and plots and assassinations among the political leaders abounded. The historical situation at the time Hosea was ministering was probably soon after the death of Pekahiah, or between Pekah and Hoshea which would have been at the time when the Assyrian Empire was expanding westward. Damascus fell in 732 BC and northern parts of Israel were occupied. Political anarchy and intrigues within Israel were rife, hence the cynical comment, *"Even if we had a king what could he do for us?"*

From verse 5 Hosea turns to Bethel which he loved to call 'Beth Aven', house of wickedness. He foresees its destruction by the Assyrians. They will take the golden calf that had stood there for the past 200 years and parade it as a tribute to the king of Assyria which will be a disgrace to the people of Israel. *"The high places of wickedness will be destroyed – it is the sin of Israel."* This, no doubt, was a pronouncement that Hosea would have felt to have been thoroughly deserved as the judgement of God that had been pending since the days of Jeroboam I and his revolt against Rehoboam.

It will not only be Bethel, but the monarchy of Israel will also be destroyed by the Assyrians. *"Samaria and its king float away like a twig on the surface of the waters."* The monarchy had been responsible for the religious policy of the nation for the past 200 years and they had allowed 'high places of wickedness' to be established in the land. This is the sin of Israel that will soon come to an end with the destruction that is going to fall upon Israel. The high places will be overrun by thorns and thistles, and this will be such a disaster that the people will cry out to the mountains, *"Cover us!"* And to the hills, *"Fall on us."* These were words that Jesus quoted on his way to the cross (Lk 23:30).

Hosea then returns to the days of Gibeah when so many men of Benjamin were killed in the terrible events in Judges 19. The sin of those days cast a lasting shame upon the nation that had never been cleansed. The punishment of Yahweh was about to fall upon the people of Israel that would be a just reward for all their sins.

The final word in this section in verse 11 returns to the agricultural metaphor of the land being threshed. A yoke will be put upon the neck of both Ephraim and Judah that will break up the hard ground where there had been no repentance, but this will be part of the justice of God for all their sins.

18 BREAK UP UNPLOUGHED GROUND
Hosea 10:11-15

Sow for yourselves righteousness, reap the fruit of unfailing love, and break up your unploughed ground, for it is time to seek the Lord, until he comes and showers righteousness on you.

This final word in the previous sector had been part of an agricultural metaphor which is continued in this section where we return to verse 11. Ephraim and Judah are called upon to break up the hard ground which is something that usually happened just after Tabernacles and the harvest celebrations. The hard ground had to be broken up so that the rain could soak into the ground, softening it up ready for seed to be sown.

In this metaphor, Israel is depicted as a mature heifer who enjoys threshing, but there were two kinds of threshing at that time. What is being referred to here is the easy task of threshing the gathered corn where the heifer went round and round separating the wheat from the chaff on the threshing floor. In Deuteronomy 25:4 the regulation is laid down that the ox should not be muzzled when threshing but should be allowed to eat grain whilst doing the job. By allowing this the farmer was acting justly, which helps us to understand God's view of justice.

The second kind of threshing was more demanding of strength to pull a plough over rock-hard ground to break it up after a long dry summer. This was really hard work and the animal had to be driven to accomplish it.

Israel was now being commanded to do a hard task – to break up the hard spiritual ground that had not been changed by repentance for two centuries! This was the final call for repentance and change, calling for 'sowing righteousness' which would reap the 'fruit of unfailing love'. Judah also was included in this command to break up her hard ground. Many biblical scholars think that this is a later addition to Hosea's text. Of course, we know that Hosea's ministry was in the last days of the monarchy in Israel before the Assyrian invasion and the destruction of Samaria and Bethel, and we know that his words could only have been preserved by being taken to

Jerusalem. Nevertheless, there are many times when Hosea does include Judah and there seems no reason to doubt that this is one of them, written by Hosea.

The call, *"For it is time to seek the Lord,"* could have come at any time and it would surely apply to both kingdoms. Judah was also in need of repentance because Ahaz was on the throne and he was far from being a godly king. He went to Damascus in the third year of the reign of Hoshea in Samaria and did a deal with Tiglath-Pileser of Assyria which he also sealed by erecting an altar in the temple in Jerusalem to one of the pagan gods of Assyria (2 Kgs 16:10). If Hosea had got word of this, he would surely have been calling for repentance in Judah!

One of the things that always happened at Tabernacles was to pray for rain that was essential to ensure the germination of the seeds of the new crop for next year's harvest. Of course, the ground had to be broken up before the rain came or it would simply run off the surface and not soften the soil. The unploughed ground of sinful Israel had to be broken up before the refreshing showers of righteousness came, that God would shower upon them if they repented.

Hosea's word was falling upon the hard unbroken ground upon which Israel had planted wickedness and reaped evil. They had eaten the fruit of deception because they believed that the nation was secure from any enemy attack. Jeroboam II had been responsible for this deception. He openly boasted about the strength of the fortifications he had put on around the major cities of Israel and he declared that Samaria with its natural defences was secure from any attack. He also boasted about the strength of his army and the number of chariots that he had. His trust was certainly not in the God of Israel, and this lay behind Hosea's indictment, *"you have depended on your own strength."*

What God was looking for was love and trust. This had been absent in the land of Israel at least for the past two centuries. Now the day of reckoning was coming when the people of Israel would desperately need the power of God for protection against the Assyrians. We have no idea of the identity of Shalman or Beth Arbel as they are not mentioned elsewhere in the Bible or in secular literature, but Hosea's prophecy of the destruction of Bethel and the overthrow of Israel was certainly fulfilled in 722 BC.

19 GOD'S LOVE FOR ISRAEL   Hosea 11:1-7

When Israel was a child I loved him, and out of Egypt I called my son. But the more I called Israel, the further they went from me. They sacrificed to the Baals and they burned incense to images.

This is one of the best loved Scriptures in the Bible. Its message is at the heart of the book of Hosea revealing vital truths about the love and justice of God. There are three parts in this chapter: verses 1 to 4 deal with the past, verses 5 to 7 deal with the present and verses 8 to 11 deal with the future and God's intention to redeem Israel. We will deal with the first two parts in this study.

There are two passages in this chapter that provide the Torah background to the subject. They are found in Deuteronomy 13:6-11 and 21:18-21 where the problems of idolatry and a rebellious son are dealt with. In 11:1 Hosea sets the scene. Israel was in slavery in Egypt and God responded to his cries and redeemed him. The statement, *"Out of Egypt I called my son"* could have been misunderstood in Hosea's day when some pagan religions regarded their deity as literally having fathered them. For this reason, Hosea used the Hebrew verb *kara* meaning 'to call' but literally 'to call into a bond or relationship' – called for a purpose.

The best way of understanding this word is seen in the English Nonconformist Churches where a minister is not appointed by a bishop – he is 'called' by members of a local church who issue 'a call' to him or her to become their pastor. The concept of 'a calling' became a social value during the Victorian era in Britain and was still part of the culture at the middle of the twentieth century. It was quite common for young people to respond to a 'calling' upon their life to enter one of the caring professions such as medicine or nursing. They believed they were serving God through responding to such a 'call'. It was quite common to hear people speak about 'a call' upon their lives – a concept which was derived from Hosea's use of the term *kara* – 'to call for a purpose'.

God saw the condition of the people of Israel in Egypt and *'called'* them to come to him at Mount Sinai where he established a covenant relationship with them – binding them to him in a relationship of love, loyalty, and trust.

Sadly, the people of Israel did not remain loyal to God. When they reached the land he had promised them instead of destroying the high places of the Canaanites they worshipped their Baals, offering sacrifices to idols. This was more than an act of disloyalty; it was a demonstration of the central tragedy in the history of Ephraim – they never understood what God had done for them.

The children of Israel were infants in Egypt, but when God called them, they came together as a nation and God had to teach them to move from infancy to youth in the wilderness and to prepare them for adulthood (maturity) when they reached Canaan and were exposed to all the temptations of the world. God led them through the wilderness with *"cords of human kindness"* and with *"ties of love"*, providing for all their needs – food and water, and protection from their enemies; but they did not understand what God had done for them.

The second part of verse 4 presents enormous difficulties in translating the Hebrew. Most English Bibles follow the KJV in seeing this as an agricultural metaphor lifting the yoke from an animal's mouth to enable it to feed. Recent archaeological findings reveal something quite different. Reading *al* for *ol* we get 'baby' instead of 'yoke', giving an act of comforting a distressed child, such as a mother lifting a baby to her face to comfort a crying infant. A literal translation is: *"I was to them like those who lift a baby to their cheek: I bent down to them that I might feed them."* It is a beautiful picture of the gentle, caring, love of God for his people – a love that tragically was never understood.

Verses 5 to 7 speak of what Hosea could foresee would happen when Assyria invaded the land with their swords flashing in every town and city across Israel. This would be the inevitable punishment for the sins of Israel in deserting their God and turning to idolatry. They would return to the state in which they were living in Egypt – a state of slavery, oppressed by the cruelty of the Assyrians in the same way as they were by the Egyptians. All this was because the people of Israel were determined to turn away from their God.

20 THE DILEMMA FACING GOD   Hosea 11:8-11

How can I give you up, Ephraim? How can I hand you over, Israel? How can I treat you like Admah? How can I make you like Zeboiim? My heart is changed within me; all my compassion is aroused.

Hosea reaches into the very heart of God in this passage. In his times of intercession, Hosea senses the clash between love and justice in God. Both are equal parts of the nature of God. The difficulty of understanding this passage starts in the first word, *'How'* which can be translated either as a question or an exclamation, as in Lamentations 1:1, *"How deserted lies the city, once so full of people!*

This passage should not be read as questions but as exclamations, as in Lamentations. God is not asking a question but is expressing dismay at the inevitable judgement coming upon Israel for their disloyalty, thereby putting themselves outside his loving protection. This is an expression of sorrow rather than God questioning whether or not to carry out the sentence required in the Torah for a disobedient son.

Admah and Zeboiim which were destroyed with Sodom and Gomorrah (Deut 29:23) are an indication of the destruction that would come upon Israel. This actually happened when the Assyrians transported whole communities and scattered them across their Empire, bringing others in to repopulate the land of Israel. This was, indeed, the end of the northern kingdom of Israel, creating the Samaritans who were there in the time of Jesus.

The next statement, *"My heart is changed within me; all my compassion is aroused,"* has caused considerable discussion among biblical scholars. This reads as though God was actually changing his mind and declining to carry out the required punishment. The Septuagint says, *"My heart is thrown into confusion",* which is surely something that Hosea would never have said about God! God is never in confusion!

Verse 9 appears to reverse the decision to inflict punishment as demanded by the law. The punishment for idolatry was, *"stone him to death"* (Deut 13:10). Similarly, in the case of a rebellious son, the parents had to go to the elders at the gate and make their accusation.

If the boy was found guilty, he had to be stoned by all the men of the town. This was the justice that faced Israel (Deut 21:18-21).

Certainly, Hosea was sensing the dismay in God's heart at what he knew was coming to Israel. He was deeply troubled, but there was hope. Hosea's ministry was to the **whole house of Israel** which included Judah and what he foresaw was the redeemed people of Israel who would emerge after judgement had fallen upon **both Israel and Judah**. This is of immense importance.

God is never taken by surprise. He knew what was coming upon his people. He saw the outcome of judgement upon both houses of Israel which would establish the 'new covenant' later foreseen by Jeremiah (31:31) and the resurrection of the nation as the new Israel foreseen by Ezekiel in the valley of the dry bones (Ezek 37).

What is being seen here as hesitation and confusion in God is quite wrong. Hosea discovered that God is never confused but he is perfectly capable of holding two polar opposite concepts in his hands at the same time – without confusion! Love and justice coalesce in the purposes of God resulting in something beyond human comprehension. This is why God exclaims, *"For I am God, and not man – the holy one among you!"* Israel was bringing judgement upon themselves, but God would not allow that to wipe Israel out – the justice of God is quite different from that of humanity. As God said to Isaiah, *"My thoughts are not your thoughts, neither are your ways my ways"* (Is 55:8). Hosea was thinking on an entirely different plane.

He saw hope in the midst of destruction. That hope would be like the roar of a lion that brings her cubs running to her side. Calling them, not driving them away! He foresaw the redeemed remnant coming back to their land as one united people as Jeremiah foresaw. *"The days are coming . . . when I will bring my people Israel and Judah back from captivity and restore them to the land"* (Jer 30:3). They would rebuild shattered settlements as Ezekiel foresaw, *"Towns will be inhabited and the ruins rebuilt"* (Ezek 36:10).

The restoration of Israel and Judah in the last days after the dispersion among the nations will not just be the return of survivors from Assyria and Babylon who would come from the East. It is of great significance that Hosea foresees the great return of the people of Israel coming from the West! Is this what began in 1948 with the modern state of Israel? Could it pave the way for the *'One new man'* of Eph 2:15?

21 THE TREACHERY OF ISRAEL
Hosea 11:12 – 12:6

Ephraim has surrounded me with lies, the house of Israel with deceit. And Judah is unruly against God, even against the faithful Holy One of God.

We are following the Hebrew Bible in this passage where chapter 12 begins at what we have in our English translations at 11:12. It begins with the charge of deception and lies, that the northern kingdom of Israel has practised before God for a long period in its history. In a similar manner Judah had been unfaithful and rebellious towards God. This meant that the whole house of Israel had not been faithful to God for a very long time.

This charge of unfaithfulness was to be seen in the foreign policy pursued by both kingdoms. Neither Ephraim nor Judah put their trust in the God of Israel. Each of them sought to make agreements with foreign powers. They thought that their security lay in their diplomacy through which they made treaties of support with Gentile nations who served bits of wood and stone as their gods.

These treaties were highly dangerous as illustrated by the phrase, *"He pursues the east wind all day."* The east wind was notoriously bad for Judah and Israel because it was a scorching hot wind that blew from the desert and destroyed the crops on the ground. In a bad year all the vegetation would suffer and what began as luscious growth promising an abundant harvest soon became starved of water and burnt to a cinder by the fierce heat of the wind.

Hosea used this as an example of the danger to the future of both Israel and Judah in making treaties with Assyria or Babylon. Both of them were enemies of the people of Israel and no good could come from making a treaty with either of them. These foreign empires would prove to be the downfall of the people of Israel who had turned their backs upon the one true God. Hosea saw this in legal terms that Yahweh was bringing a charge against those with whom he had entered into a covenant relationship to protect them, provided they remained faithful and loyal to him, worshipping no foreign god.

The justice of God demanded that he would leave them to their fate which was the inevitable outcome of their ways. Hosea then used the traditions that had been handed down to him through the centuries of the lies and deception that had been in the character of Jacob, the ancestor of both Israel and Judah. They both had these same characteristics of being untrustworthy. Jacob's character could be seen even in the womb where he tried to supplant his brother which was why he was given the name of Jacob, (Hebrew *ya-aqob*) "*he grasped his brother's heel*" (Gen 25:26). He had coveted his brother's birthright and stolen his father's blessing. But there had been a great change in Jacob when he repented of his sins and struggled with God at the ford of the river Jabbok (Gen 32:22). Following his repentance he was given a new name, 'Israel' – Hebrew, *yisra el* to 'strive with God' (Gen 35:10).

Jacob had always striven for God's blessing and when he struggled with God, or with an angel of God, his life was changed. This encounter with God that changed his name was at Bethel where his descendants, the northern kingdom of Israel, had set up a golden calf which they worshipped.

This was the sin which they had been committing since the days of Jeroboam I. Yet it was here at Bethel that the name of 'Yahweh' was revealed (Hebrew YHWH – vowels are never included in the name). Instead of destroying the Canaanite high places Israel had done the most terrible thing in installing their own idol, a golden calf, saying that this was the God who had brought them up out of Egypt. They thus desecrated what had been a holy place where Jacob had met God.

The final verse in this section is of great significance. Hosea pleads with the nation to return to their own God. If they would return to God, maintaining loving-kindness (Hebrew *chesed*) and justice, putting their trust in God and waiting for him, he would undoubtedly respond to them.

The reference here about waiting for the Lord God is a link back to the dying wishes of Jacob. When he was on his deathbed, he called his sons together to bless them, looking at the character of each of them before framing his blessing. His final prayer to God for himself was, "*I look for your deliverance Lord*" or, more literally, "*I wait for your salvation O God*" (Gen 49:18). Hosea applies this to the people of Israel, pleading with them to put their trust in the Lord and wait for his deliverance.

22 THE INDICTMENT OF ISRAEL   Hosea 12:7-14

The merchant uses dishonest scales; he loves to defraud. Ephraim boasts, I am very rich, I have become wealthy. With all my wealth they will not find in me any iniquity or sin.

This passage sounds much more like Amos than Hosea. It is, of course, possible that Hosea had access to some of Amos' notes as he followed in his footsteps just a few years later. Hosea must have said this during the period of turmoil around the monarchy following the death of Jeroboam II and after the assassination of his son six months later.

Jeroboam's 40-year reign produced the kind of wealth that Hosea was referring to in 12:8. He clearly was aware of the lack of integrity and the *"dishonest scales"* that was the driving force behind the so-called wealth of the nation. Amos had referred to this in his review of the practices in the marketplace where traders cheated housewives by *"skimping the measure, boosting the price and cheating"* (Am 8:5).

Those practices were only the tip of the iceberg because the merchants of Israel had become known worldwide for their sharp practices. These had been developed over many years. Hosea calls Ephraim a 'merchant' which was a reputation that had been built up since the days when the Canaanites occupied the land. They were known as merchants (Hebrew *canaan*) which stretched back to their origins in the land around Babylon where Babylon was known as the 'city of merchants'.

This boasting about wealth and power did not impress God, especially as they were using it as a sign of his blessing upon the people of Israel – showing that they had no *"iniquity or sin"*; they were in a right relationship with God – or so they thought! Hosea disputes this with a direct word from God, *"I am the Lord your God who brought you out of Egypt, I will make you live in tents again, as in the days of your appointed feasts."*

One of the appointed feasts would have been 'Tabernacles' when the people had to live in booths in the desert. There is an important word here that is relevant for all time; that the acquisition of wealth should not be used as a sign of blessing from God! There are plenty of crooked merchants in every generation! There can also be crooked religious leaders! The threat in this statement was that God would reduce Israel to the same state as they were in when Moses led them through the desert.

The next verse reminded them of their spiritual heritage – that God had spoken to the people of Israel in every generation through the prophets whom he had sent to them to instruct them and to guide them. Jeremiah picked up this same point; he heard God saying, *"From the time your forefathers left Egypt until now, day after day, again and again I sent you my servants the prophets. But they did not listen to me"* (Jer 7:25).

In the final verses of chapter 12 Hosea goes back to the Jacob connection with Bethel. He notes how Jacob had fled the promised land and run to Syria in order to find a wife. Then he had had to pay for her by tending sheep for his father-in-law Laban, but God had given the land of Canaan to his people Israel as a free gift. He had also given them prophets who led them from slavery to the promised land. He had actually spoken to them through visions and parables – even revealing his name to Moses, which had not been given to any other nation.

The Gilgal reference shows the scorn with which God looked upon the golden calf at Bethel. It was nothing more than a 'heap of stones' (Hebrew *gal*) like Jacob and Laban had erected at Bethel in the names of their respective gods (Gen 31:46). But Israel was now rejecting all the truth that had been revealed by the prophets and what God had done for them in bringing them out of Egypt. Their ingratitude compounded by bloodshed over the centuries was now provoking the anger of the Lord. They were bringing upon themselves the inevitable punishment for their sinfulness.

The contempt that they had displayed towards the God who loved them was indescribable. He had used the Prophet Moses to rescue the people from slavery in Egypt and through him he had given his teaching and established his covenant with his people, but all this free gift from the Lord had been ignored by the people of Israel. The penalty for this treachery was that God would now leave Israel to face the future of their guilt. Israel had rejected the Lord the Redeemer, and now would have to face the consequences of their blood guilt and the justice of the Lord.

23 THE LORD'S ANGER AGAINST ISRAEL
Hosea 13:1-8

When Ephraim spoke, men trembled; he was exalted in Israel. But he became guilty of Baal worship and died. Now they sin more and more, they make idols for themselves from their silver.

Chapter 13 has four sections, verses 1-3; 4-8; 9-13; and 14-16. In this study we are covering the first two sections. The first section looks back at the past and the second section looks at the present. The opening statement that Ephraim was exalted refers to the history of the tribes. In Genesis 48 we read of Joseph taking his two sons Manasseh and Ephraim to see their grandfather Jacob who was dying. Joseph presented his two sons for a blessing, but instead of recognising Manasseh as the firstborn, Jacob crossed his arms when he had the two boys in front of him, putting his right hand on Ephraim's head although he was the younger, and putting his left hand on Manasseh's head, even though Manasseh was the firstborn (Gen 48:14).

This prime status of Ephraim was recognised among the tribes in the settlement in Canaan. Joshua himself was an Ephraimite and Jeroboam I who led the revolt against Rehoboam and founded the northern state of Israel was also an Ephraimite. His word was law in Israel, hence the saying that he was exalted. But Jeroboam did not want his people going up to Jerusalem, so he established Bethel as the national shrine.

Sadly, Jeroboam installed a golden calf and led Israel into idolatry. The phrase, *"He became guilty of Baal worship and died"* does not mean physical death, but spiritual death. He died to the truth of the God of Israel and set the nation on course for eventual termination. They continued in idolatry, making silver replicas of the golden calf for household gods. There is even mention here of human sacrifice which is referred to in 2 Kings 17:17.

They did, however, engage in a multiplicity of idolatry as recorded in 2 Kings 23 when Josiah carried out his purge of the whole land of Israel after the discovery of the 'Book of the Law' during the temple repairs. It is an astonishing record showing the amount of idolatry that was housed in the temple in Jerusalem. It even refers to *"the quarters of the male shrine prostitutes, which were in the temple of the Lord where the women did weaving for Asherah"* (2 Kings 23:7). Josiah even went to Bethel and tore down the altar and high places there which he burned and ground to powder (2 Kings 23:15). Hosea was evidently foreseeing this destruction. He speaks of the worship at Bethel disappearing like early morning dew or like the dust of chaff or smoke from a fire.

This theme of destruction is continued in the second section, verses 4-8 where Hosea reminds the people of Israel of their own history which they had evidently either forgotten or deliberately ignored. *"I am the Lord your God who brought you out of Egypt"* which was followed by the first commandment, *"You shall acknowledge no God but me."* There was no statement more important than this in the history of Israel. It was there in the Torah, and it had been taught to successive generations of children since the days of Moses. *"These commandments that I give you today are to be in your hearts. Impress them on your children. Talk about them when you sit at home and when you walk along the road"* (Deut 6:6).

Hosea then summarises the message that was at the heart of his ministry. *"When I fed them, they were satisfied; when they were satisfied, they became proud, then they forgot me."* The pathos in this statement is clear. The love and generosity that God had lavished upon his people was simply accepted as their right, but never acknowledged with thankfulness.

This, of course, is the story of humanity, summarised in the history of Israel, the Lord's chosen people, who were in a covenant relationship with him. Moses had warned the people quite clearly of what would happen if they broke the covenant. There was no excuse for ignorance of these consequences. Hosea reiterates them, saying that God's patience will finally break and when he does act he will be like the combination of the ferocity of a lion, the swiftness of a leopard and the fierce anger of a mother bear robbed of her cubs.

The love and justice of God are brought together in this combination. God had given every possible warning to his children. His love and grief are seen together – when he fed his people, instead of responding in loving gratitude, they became proud and forgot him – the divine tragedy is seen here.

24 RANSOM AND REDEMPTION   Hosea 13:9-16

You are destroyed, O Israel, because you are against me, against your helper. Where is your king, that he may save you? Where are your rulers in all your towns?

Hosea had already described the guilt of Israel. He returns to the subject today emphasising that the guilt is there, right through the nation from the king to the rulers and to the people. In the early days of the settlement in Canaan the people demanded to have a king so that they could be like all the nations. This was a revolt against Yahweh the God of Israel who was their king and their leader who would guide them and protect them.

This desire to be like the nations provoked the anger of God when it first emerged in the time of the Prophet Samuel when he was an old man, and the people asked for a king. God's response was, *"It is not you they have rejected, but they have rejected me as their king"* (1 Sam 8:7). This same desire to be like the Gentile nations was there among the exiles in Babylon which Ezekiel had to face. He said this would never happen as he heard God saying, *"As surely as I live, declares the Sovereign Lord, I will rule over you with a mighty hand and an outstretched arm and with outpoured wrath"* (Ezek 20:33).

Two things were of supreme importance in God's relationship with his people: he wanted to see absolute loyalty, and trust. The two were tightly bound together and they sealed the binding relationship that had been formed at Mount Sinai. This was never understood by the people of Israel. The height of their disaffection was reached by Jeroboam I when he split from Judah after the death of King Solomon and he installed the golden calf at Bethel telling the people that this was the God of Israel who had led them out of Egypt.

God was deeply hurt by this as we see from Hosea's revelation in chapter 13: *"When I fed them they were satisfied; when they were satisfied, they became proud, then they forgot me."* Hosea, in his marriage was grieving at his own broken relationship with his wife, but he saw this as just a tiny reflection of the suffering in the heart of God over his wayward people Israel, to whom he had entrusted the knowledge of his name and with whom he had established a binding covenant of love and faithfulness.

Verses 12 and 13 express the guilt of Ephraim being the lack of wisdom – they had not even got the basic understanding of what constituted a covenant relationship of love and trust which should have been part of their received humanity since they were created in the image of God. Ephraim was like an unborn child who did not respond to the cycle of birth pangs and leave the womb – he was so stupid that he could not even understand the free gift of God's love, the response to which should come naturally.

Verse 14 presents a problem, the statement *"I will ransom them from the power of the grave"* sounds very similar to sentiments in 11:8-9 where God was wrestling with the clash of love and justice, *"How can I give you up Ephraim!"* But this is followed by statements, *"Where, O death, are your plagues? Where, O grave, is your destruction?"* It is difficult to know whether this is a positive statement or a threat.

The difficulty for Christians is compounded by the fact that St Paul quotes this verse in support of his belief in the resurrection of Christ – *"Death has been swallowed up in victory"* (1 Cor 15:54). Paul obviously believes it to be a positive promise of redemption, but our difficulty in interpreting Hosea's meaning is complicated by it being followed by *"I will have no compassion."*

Hosea clearly was foreseeing the onslaught of the Assyrian army and the terrible things that they would do in Samaria and in the towns and cities of Israel where even little children would be struck by their swords. The east wind blowing from the desert was said to be coming from the Lord, meaning that it was his will that Israel should now suffer for their years of faithlessness and idolatry. But the statement, *"I will ransom them from the power of the grave"* was a messianic hope that was fulfilled through the life and death and resurrection of Jesus. This is a messianic prophecy. We learn this from the word translated 'compassion' – Hebrew *nocham* which comes from the verb *nacham* meaning 'repentance'. From this we see Hosea's belief that the coming disaster would eventually bring the salvation of Israel – transforming repentance into salvation – which prepares the way for the final chapter.

25 REPENTANCE, SALVATION AND BLESSING
Hosea 14:1-9

Return O Israel, to the Lord your God. Your sins have been your downfall! Take words with you and return to the Lord.

This final chapter has a little summary of the message that Hosea has been bringing to the people of Israel. It is a mixture of love, justice, grace, and the sovereignty of God, that Hosea personified in his own life, and he brings it here in his final plea to his fellow countrymen. It begins with the word *'return'* (Hebrew *shub*) that has been a constant theme in his ministry and he uses it twice here in the first two verses.

His primary theme in this final chapter is for 'confession' followed by 'forgiveness of sins'. Hosea pleads with the people to return to the Lord with prayers of confession upon their lips. He is assuming that by now the people of Israel will have realised that the Assyrians cannot help them and neither is it any use looking to the Egyptians to come on their warhorses to rescue them. Those are two facts that have to be openly confessed before the Lord. They have to renounce the idolatry that they have practised for so many years and declare that they will never again worship bits of wood and stone that they themselves have made with their own hands.

Hosea foresees such repentance being immediately received graciously by God. His anger would be turned away and his love would readily flow to embrace them. His love would be like the morning dew on the ground that waters young crops, and God's blessings would flow like the blossoms of the lily. Maybe Jesus had this promise of the Father's immediate response in his mind when he told the story about the return of the 'prodigal son' whose father rushed to enfold him in his arms and to forgive him.

Hosea sees the need for the people to return to God with prayers of repentance covering three major areas of sin – namely, first their sins of idolatry, worshipping the golden calf at Bethel and at the old Canaanite high places up in the hills of Israel. Secondly, their reliance upon making pacts and treaties with foreign nations such as Assyria and Egypt instead of putting their reliance entirely upon Yahweh the God of Israel. Thirdly, they needed to renounce their trust based upon 'war-horses' which, in this context, means putting their trust in their own army and the strength of the fortifications around their cities which had been the pride of Jeroboam II.

Hosea foresaw that the loving response of God would not only be in extending forgiveness to his wayward people, but he would send them unlimited prosperity like the cedars of Lebanon that send down deep roots to ensure the health and well-being of their trees even in times of drought. The splendour of Israel would thus be like the fragrance of a cedar forest and the people of Israel would bask in its shade.

This prosperity which would be the fruit of repentance would spread the fame of Israel across all nations and redound to the glory of God. Hosea had been teaching that it was God's intention to reveal himself to the Gentile nations through Israel and now he declares that the fruitfulness of Israel will come from him and be seen by all the world.

The final verse in this section in verse 8 is a cry from the heart of God, *"O Ephraim, what more have I to do with idols?"* This surely reflects Hosea's own unhappy marriage to a woman he loved, but she loved other men more than her husband. Hosea himself finally went and paid the price of her redemption from sin and brought her into his home to surround her with love and care. Hosea sees this as a parable of God's unbreakable love for his rebellious people.

It is quite possible that Hosea even foresaw a glimpse of the eternal purposes of God through Messiah who in his own body would pay the redemption price for sin, as Isaiah who succeeded him in the prophetic ministry two centuries later wrote, *"Surely, he took up our infirmities and carried our sorrows, yet we considered him stricken by God smitten by him and afflicted. But he was pierced for our transgressions"* (Is 53:4-5).

The little epilogue in 14.9 offers words of wisdom. Those who are wise will be given discernment. As Paul would say, *"The man without the Spirit does not accept the things that come from the Spirit of God, for they are foolishness to him, and he cannot understand them, because they are spiritually discerned"* (1 Cor 2:14). But the wise will understand the teaching and the ways of the Lord, and they will walk in them.

CONCLUSION: THE UNIQUE MESSAGE OF HOSEA

Hosea is different. It does not fit into any traditional slot in the Bible. It has a unique place among the prophets of Israel where the identity of the prophet is usually hidden – it was the word of God that was promoted by the prophets, so the identity of the messenger was of little or no importance. The name of the prophet's father was usually given, simply for identification, although both Amos and Micah's family names were omitted and they were simply identified by their hometown – *"Amos one of the shepherds of Tekoa",* and *"Micah of Moresheth".*

It was sometimes necessary to identify the family line of the prophet in order to establish his credentials in delivering a very important word, such as when Jehoshaphat was facing an overwhelming army of invasion and there was a desperate need of divine guidance: *"Then the Spirit of the Lord came upon Jahaziel son of Zechariah, the son of Benaiah, the son of Jeiel, the son of Mattaniah, a Levite and descendant of Asaph." (2 Chron 20:14)* This long family line was essential for weighing the words of prophecy on such a significant occasion. In the case of the books of Amos and Micah who clearly had a group of followers to record and a authenticate their words, their personal identity was not important and might detract from the significance of the word of God which was not from a human being however well established in the nation.

In the case of Hosea, we are simply told that he is the son of Beeri, but no other details are given, not even his hometown. The only thing we know about him is his relationship with Gomer. We are told that they had three children, and we are told their names because this is part of the prophetic story, but we are not told any details of their family life, or even where they lived. None of that is important because this is not a biography of the Hosea family life. All the focus is upon the word of the Lord directing the action of the prophet so that he could receive a unique revelation of the nature and purposes of God. The story is a living parable every bit as significant in the ministry of Hosea as was the parable of the Prodigal Son in the ministry of Jesus.

The message that Hosea was given, as we said in the Introduction, is a mixture of love, grace, justice, forgiveness, tenderness and suffering. This reflects the complexity of the nature of God. It was through the complexity of Hosea's relationship with Gomer that he came to this understanding of God. It was God who had told him to go and find Gomer and to marry her. God would have known what was going to happen, so every little bit of the relationship between the two of them was of spiritual significance enabling the prophet to understand the complexity of the nature and purposes of God which are hidden from most human beings because they can only be understood on a different spiritual plane. In the text we have quoted from the words of Isaiah 55:8, *"My thoughts are not your thoughts."* We have also quoted Paul saying, *"The man without the Spirit does not accept the things that come from the Spirit of God, for they are foolishness to him"* (1 Cor 2:14). Hosea had to learn to think on a completely different plane in order to understand the nature and purposes of God.

The height of spiritual revelation in the book of Hosea is reached in study number 20 covering Hosea 11:8-11. Hosea wrestles with the complex issue of God's relationship with the rebellious people whom he had chosen as his special people through whom he would reveal his nature and purposes to the world. They had broken the covenant and were thereby bringing judgement upon themselves. God could have intervened and this is what Hosea was permitted to observe – God wrestling with the clash of justice and love. Most of our Bibles in the Western church have wrong translations of Hosea 11:8. They put a ? instead of a ! after each statement which changes the meaning of the passage and makes it sound as though God was in a state of confusion. The great revelation of the nature of God given to Hosea was that God can hold in his hands two polar opposite concepts – with no confusion! This is because his truth can only be discerned on a different spiritual plane from those on which human beings usually operate.

Hosea's study of the history of Israel in the light of the covenant established at Mount Sinai presented a unique revelation of the nature of God, of his patience and his love, his longing to forgive and to restore the relationship that Israel had broken through their sinfulness. This presented God with the kind of dilemma faced in Chapter 11 where Hosea tries to describe the conflict of emotions between compassion and justice that God had to face. The suffering of God is also beautifully described, *"It was I who taught Ephraim to walk"* – even lifting the infant to his cheek with ties of love, but they ran after idols. This resulted in terrible suffering for God – his precious child over whom he had lavished love from birth, had scorned him. None of the other prophets achieve this level of pathos in their understanding of God that Hosea reaches. This would not have been possible without the experience of his own unfaithful marriage. God often uses the most trying circumstances in our lives to enable us to gain in spiritual understanding and truth.

Hosea's message is a mixture of love, compassion and justice which composes the 'wrath of God' that allows judgement to come upon his people as the automatic outcome of their sinful behaviour. This opens the door to cruel enemies such as the Assyrians and Babylonians who could easily have been stopped by God – who in the words of Isaiah 40:15 held the nations in his hands *"as a drop in a bucket"*. When God briefly, for a few moments abandons his people (Is 54:7-8) this is what happens, but God longs to redeem his people: *"I will not carry out my fierce anger, nor will I turn and devastate Ephraim. For I am God, not man – the Holy One among you"* (11:9).

Hosea, more than any other prophet, reaches an understanding of God that was beyond any other messenger. Isaiah recognised the problem faced by human beings in his famous statement that lies at the heart of biblical revelation, *"As the heavens are higher than the earth, so are my ways higher than your ways and my thoughts than your thoughts"* (Is 55:9). Isaiah recognises that the thoughts of God and of human beings are on an entirely different plane. Hosea gets a little closer to that plane on which God operates. He moves into a different gear and begins thinking in a different dimension through the heartbreaking experience of his own personal life, but he is only able to do that because he had already achieved such a close relationship with God that he was able to distinguish his voice, and he had learned to love and to trust the Lord so that he was able to be obedient in whatever he was told to do.

INTRODUCTION TO *TODAY WITH MICAH*

Micah the Man

Micah described himself as a man of Moresheth, a small country town near the border with Gaza. The Shephelah was a region of fertile countryside south-west of Jerusalem, guarding the route to Jerusalem from the west. Hence Rehoboam fortified Lachish which Micah describes as being in the forefront of transgression, bringing in chariots from Egypt instead of putting their trust in Yahweh the God of Israel.

We know little about the life of Micah and nothing about his family, or even his father's name or if he was married or had family. His description of the agony of a woman in childbirth (4:9-10) indicates that he has been married and had experience of family life. He clearly is a much-travelled man and knows the history of the building of Samaria by Omri and Ahab who used a special stone for which the city became famous.

Micah names the towns of the region around his hometown, seeing the greed, covetousness, and deceitfulness as the social sins of the people. Micah was not only a countryman, he knew Jerusalem and the leaders of the nation – the politicians, and the crooked judges who took bribes and denied justice to the poor. He also knew the temple community, the priests and prophets who offered personal prophecies for money. He clearly had a heart for the poor and the powerless.

Historical Background

The book of Micah states that his ministry was in the reigns of Jothan, Ahaz, and Hezekiah, kings of Judah. This covered 56 years from the beginning of Jothan to the end of Hezekiah. Jothan reigned from 742 – 735 BC and Hezekiah from 715 – 687 BC. Isaiah and Micah spanned most of this time. Isaiah started earlier than Micah, and lived to the end of Hezekiah's reign.

The peace and prosperity of the first half of the eighth century BC was interrupted by the rising power of Assyria beginning with Tiglath-Pileser in 744 BC. The fall of Damascus in 732 BC changed the face of the western Middle East. It coincided with political anarchy in Israel following the death of Jeroboam II, in 746 BC. His son Zechariah was murdered after only six months by Shallum who was assassinated one month later, followed by Menahem who surrendered to Assyria. He was succeeded by Pekah who formed an alliance to oppose Assyria.

Judah refused to join the alliance, so Pekah attacked Judah who appealed to the Assyrians for help. Pekah was murdered by Hoshea who also surrendered to the Assyrians but later rebelled, which led to the destruction of Samaria by Sargon II in 722/1 BC. This destroyed the northern kingdom of Israel, whose population was scattered around the Assyrian Empire, while other nationalities were brought into Israel and resettled. The Assyrians, now led by Sennacherib invaded Judah in 701 BC and again a few years later which was when Hezekiah and Isaiah went into the temple and spread before the Lord the threatening letter from the Assyrian leader. Their prayers led to a plague sweeping through the Assyrian army which saved Jerusalem (Is 37:36).

The Book of Micah

There are two phrases in the first verse of the book of Micah that are significant for understanding his message: *"The word of the Lord came to Micah"* and *"the vision he saw"*. The whole book presents a revelation given in a visual form indicating the way Micah received the word of God pictorially, through what he was seeing around him. This was in a similar manner to that of Isaiah, but in contrast to Hosea, the Spirit of God within him enabled him to recognise what God was saying through what he was seeing.

Jesus heard from the Father in the same way. He said that he can only do *"what he sees his Father doing"* (Jn 5:19). Jeremiah, although not receiving visions, often saw things through which God spoke to him, such as two baskets of fruit at the temple, from which he heard that the exiles in Babylon would be the faithful remnant of the nation through whom its heritage would be preserved (Jer 24:1).

The book of Micah is in two parts: chapters 1 – 5; and chapters 6 – 7 which form the second part. Most scholars believe that the two parts were written over a large number of years. The final chapter may have been written *after* the destruction of Samaria in 721 BC. Chapter 1 sets out the purpose of Yahweh, to bring judgement upon his people because of their sins. 1:2 calls upon the whole world to witness the justice of God; 1: 3-7 sets out the fate that awaits the northern kingdom of Israel, while 1:8-16 show what is going to happen to Jerusalem and the surrounding towns. Micah was foreseeing not just events in his lifetime but events covering the period of judgement from the death of Jeroboam II in 746 BC to the destruction of Jerusalem by the Babylonians in 586 BC. His prophecies were hated at the time, as he reports in 2:6, *"Do not prophesy, their prophets say. Do not prophesy about these things, disgrace will not overtake us."*

There was still a note of optimism in the nation at that time, but Micah's warnings were never heeded. Nevertheless, as events unfolded, Micah's ministry became increasingly respected. One hundred years later, in the time of Jeremiah's trial in Jerusalem, Micah's ministry was quoted (Jer 26:18). Chapter 2 sets out the spiritual sins of the nation while chapter 3 deals mainly with the social conditions and the behaviour of the leaders. Chapter 4 looks ahead and prophesies the exile in Babylon (4:10). Chapter 5 looks beyond the judgement to the fulfilment of God's purposes for the remnant.

The second part in chapters 6 and 7 has a different tone, beginning with a kind of law court examination and an appeal from God to the people of Israel to remember their history and all that God had done for their forebears. It establishes the case for the justice of God in bringing judgement upon the nation, particularly for the idolatry of turning to other gods – breaking the first commandment which brought automatic and inevitable judgement. Chapter 7 clearly reflects the disaster that had already occurred and looks beyond the wrath of God for the day of reconstruction. It ends with the declaration of mercy and compassion through which God forgives the sins of the people, restoring them into a right relationship with himself.

1 MICAH SPEAKS TO THE WORLD   Micah 1:1-4

The word of the Lord that came to Micah of Moresheth during the reigns of Jotham, Ahaz and Hezekiah, kings of Judah – the vision he saw concerning Samaria and Jerusalem.

This opening statement from Micah sets the tone for the book. He may have come from a small town in the heart of the Judaean countryside but the message he was presenting was of worldwide significance. It was to be heard by all peoples of all nations in all generations. It was a word from the Lord God himself, the Sovereign Lord of Creation, and therefore the message demanded full attention.

The opening verse states that Micah received this word from God during the reigns of Jotham, Ahaz and Hezekiah, kings of Judah. It is strange that he makes no mention of the kings of the northern kingdom of Israel although his message is directed towards both Samaria and Jerusalem, so why does he only name the kings of Jerusalem and ignore the kings of Samaria? We are told that Micah himself was a Judaean, coming from the south of the country where he would have had little contact with the people of Israel, although from the content of his message he clearly had considerable knowledge of the situation in Israel.

It may be that his familiarity with the tumultuous political situation in Israel following the death of Jeroboam II in 747 BC when there had been a succession of kings and assassinations, caused him to want nothing to do with those sordid events. He would rather not even refer to them.

Micah claims to have received his divine message through a vision which he saw. This does not necessarily mean that he saw the words written like writing on the wall. It simply means that he was a 'seeing prophet' like Isaiah and Amos, who saw things pictorially or in visions, rather than conceptually like Hosea and Jeremiah each of whom heard the word of God delivered to them.

Micah claims to have received a vision of God coming down from his heavenly dwelling and coming to the high places of the earth. The term 'high places' usually refers to shrines with altars for the worship of idols, so this may be the prelude to the pronouncement of judgement which is why he sees the mountains melt and the valleys split apart. This is intended to convey a sense of awe that the Almighty God of Creation is the one who is speaking to all the peoples on earth and observing what they are doing. He is watching to see the activities of human beings so that he could be a righteous witness against humanity.

This opening statement uses the metaphor of a court of law in which witnesses are called and evidence is presented. This is then critically examined before judgement is given. It was a regular practice in those times for legal officials who were presenting evidence for the consideration of the court to call upon heaven and earth as witnesses to the truthfulness of the evidence they would be presenting.

This is what Micah was doing. He was establishing his credentials, that he had been sent by Almighty God to deliver a message to the peoples of the earth that they needed to hear. It was not a message that he himself had devised but it was a message that had been revealed to him by the Sovereign Lord who himself was a witness of the things that human beings were doing.

There can be no doubt that, although Micah does not identify the kings of Israel by name, he shared the view of the people of Judah that the rightful king of the people of Israel was the line of David that was continued through Rehoboam and the kings of Judah in Jerusalem. The people of Judah believed the greatest sin of Israel was committed by Jeroboam who led the 10 tribes of Israel into sin by setting up shrines in Dan and Bethel. He had installed a figure of a golden bull and told the people that this was the God of Israel who had brought them out of Egypt.

It was not only in Bethel and Dan that there were high places, but throughout the land the high places of the Canaanites had been used by people of Israel for worshipping the local Baal, while at the same time acknowledging Yahweh the God of Israel. Micah sees this as breaking the covenant by worshipping other gods and this is why God was treading upon the high places and crushing the mountains beneath his feet as a prelude to his judgement upon the peoples of the earth and upon his own people of Israel and Judah.

2 JUDGEMENT ON SAMARIA   Micah 1:5-7

All this is because of Jacob's transgression, because of the sins of the house of Israel. What is Jacob's transgression? Is it not Samaria? What is Judah's high place? Is it not Jerusalem?

Micah foresees divine judgement coming upon both Samaria and Jerusalem for their heinous sins. Judgement was coming upon the high places that were originally places of idolatry set up by the Canaanites, but these had been occupied by the people of Israel who continued worshipping at the local Canaanites' shrines while also acknowledging the God of Israel which infuriated the prophets. These practices continued for generation after generation and were officially encouraged in the northern kingdom of Israel after the division caused by Jeroboam I after his revolt against Rehoboam.

Jeroboam had not only established Bethel and Dan as the two major sanctuaries of Israel rivalling Jerusalem, but he had appointed priests who were not Levites and he had encouraged the use of other high places up in the hills. These practices developed under successive kings and under the reign of Jeroboam II the nation was steeped in places of idolatry. It was a time of luxury for the rich and oppression of the powerless. The record in 2 Kings 14:26 is that *"the Lord had seen how bitterly everyone in Israel, whether slave or free, was suffering; there was no-one to help them."* The record continues to celebrate the military achievements of Jeroboam, but as Amos observed, *"They sell the righteous for silver and the needy for a pair of sandals. They trample on the heads of the poor"* (Am 2: 6-7).

Prosperity had begun in the time of King Jehoash who had attacked Judah and taken gold and silver and other treasures from the temple in Jerusalem to his royal palace in Samaria (2 Kings 14:14). His predecessors, Omri and Ahab had laid the foundation for prosperity in the nation. Omri had purchased the land on which he had established the city of Samaria – the name was based upon the name of Shemer who was the former owner of the hill according to 1 Kings 16:24.

Micah's prophecy that Samaria would be reduced to rubble and that her stones would be poured out into the valley was a reference to the beautiful stones that Omri and Ahab had used in building the palace. Samaria was famous for its beautiful architecture and masonry which Micah says will all be destroyed and its foundations which had been laid upon idolatry would be exposed to the world as they would be broken in pieces.

There was evidently a temple in Samaria alongside the palace for the use of royalty, although according to Amos 7:13 Bethel was 'the king's sanctuary'. The whole land of Samaria was scattered with places of worship for the multitude of idols that were available to the people. The prophecy in 1:7 that all the idols would be broken and the temple gifts burnt with fire was literally fulfilled by the invasion of the Assyrians and their systematic destruction, not only of the city of Samaria but also of Bethel and other high places. Micah undoubtedly foresaw the rise of Assyria and he showed some knowledge of their tactics and he saw the hand of the God of Israel using the armies of Assyria for carrying out his judgement upon the idolatry of the people of Israel.

Micah's reference, *"she gathered her gifts from the wages of prostitutes"* is highly revealing. The type of idolatry practised at a lot of the former Canaanite shrines was based upon a form of sympathetic magic in which acts of sexual intercourse with a shrine prostitute simulated the fertility that was required of the agricultural land or of the womb of the idolatrous worshipper. The worshipper would pay for the services of the shrine prostitute, either male or female, and the money raised by these activities would be used in the initial construction of the shrine, the provision of its implements and the maintenance of its staff.

Micah rightly foresaw what was going to happen in the Assyrian invasion. Assyrian records show that Sargon took the gold and silver and ivory and other valuable commodities from the temple of the gods of Samaria and used them as offerings to his own gods in his temples in Assyria. Thus, the words of Micah were literally fulfilled.

Micah's prediction was that in the same way as gifts for the idolatrous practices of the people of Israel had been used in Samaria, they would also be used in that same way as the wages of prostitutes in Assyria. All this outpouring of wrath and destruction upon the land and the people of Israel was because of the sins of the house of Israel, described as *"Jacob's transgression"*.

3 JUDGEMENT UPON JERUSALEM   Micah 1:8-16

Because of this I will weep and wail; I will go about barefoot and naked. I will howl like a jackal and moan like an owl. For her wound is incurable; it has come to Judah. It has reached the very gate of my people, even to Jerusalem itself.

Micah is grief stricken because of what he has seen in Samaria and the way that the sins of the people of Israel had spread to Judah like a cancer spreading through the body. It had even reached the gates of Jerusalem. He repeats the words of David, *"Tell it not in Gath"*, when David did not want the Philistines rejoicing over the death of Saul. The sin of the people of Israel was so great that Micah felt the shame which he did not want to be seen by the Gentile nations of the world.

The humiliation that Micah foresaw for both the northern and the southern kingdoms of Israel was the inevitable result of their sinfulness. It was so severe that he could do no other than wail in lament because, if there was not widespread repentance in the nation, he knew that the end result was going to be national disaster.

Micah could foresee the terrible suffering of people of the Shephelah – the lowland region in the centre of southern Israel between the coastland and the hill country around Jerusalem. This was an area that was steeped in the history of Israel where many battles had been fought between the people of Israel and the Philistines. It was the area around his own hometown of Moresheth where he was born and had spent most of his life.

Micah names nine towns that were all part of the Shephelah and it is easy to see his personal grief which is the mark of the true prophet who reflects the grief of God in pronouncing judgement upon the people he loved. Micah could perceive spiritual significance in the name of each of the nine towns. He could foresee Beth Ophrah (house of dust) becoming a symbol of the people rolling in dust or parading shamefully naked as they go into exile.

Micah could foresee the invasion of the Assyrians and town after town falling to the enemy. He could see the suffering of citizens in

Maroth, which in Hebrew is a pun for 'bitter', which, prophetically he could see as judgement coming down from the Lord. He then turned his attention to Lachish which was the major city of the area and was heavily fortified with strong city walls and a permanent garrison that was the pride of the whole region.

Lachish had been fortified by Rehoboam after his split with Jeroboam I and it was the first place in Judah to adopt horse-drawn chariots for use in war similar to those of the Egyptian army. The eighth century prophets saw the horse-drawn chariot as a symbol of 'sinfulness' – hence the statement in verse 13, *"You were the beginning of sin to the Daughter of Zion."*

The transgression of Lachish was pride, which led to boasting in human strength and not trusting in God. Micah believed that their pride would lead to their downfall because the Assyrian army would defeat them which would be a judgement sent by God. Micah could foresee the leaders of Lachish mounting their chariots and fleeing away from the city when the Assyrians launched their onslaught.

Moresheth Gath sounded like 'possessions' which Micah saw as being taken away by the Assyrians who would strip the town of their wealth which would be like "*parting gifts*" taken by the enemy. Achzib was the next town, which in Hebrew was a pun for 'deception'. It was a town famous for industry that had contributed immensely to the prosperity of the nation and its businessmen were renowned across the region. All this wealth was deceptive, and Micah could foresee their industry being destroyed by the Assyrians who would come like conquerors overturning everything in the life of the nation.

The glory of Israel would be reduced to the kind of situation that faced David when he was on the run from King Saul. He hid in the cave of Adullam. The account in 1 Samuel 22:2 says, "*all those who were in distress or in debt or discontented gathered round him, and he became their leader.*" That was the sort of disorientated remnant that Micah was foreseeing would be left in the nation by the Assyrian invasion. This would all be the outcome of the sinfulness of the people of Israel, because God would no longer protect the nation that had turned its back upon Yahweh their God. They should shave their heads and go into mourning for those who were going to be taken into exile.

4 PLANS FOR THE FUTURE   Micah 2:1-5

Woe to those who plan iniquity, to those who plot evil on their beds! At morning's light they carry it out because it is in their power to do it. They covet fields and seize them, and houses, and take them.

The first two verses give a glimpse of the social situation in both Israel and Judah where a prolonged period of peace on the international scene had resulted in a growth of industry and a greatly enlarged economy. Businessmen had become a dominant factor in society involved in both national trade and in developing links widely across the Western region of nations and through links with the Phoenicians and their settlements around the Mediterranean. Prosperity was evident everywhere in towns and cities and among prominent landowners.

Together with this prosperity went the inevitable driving forces of greed and the acquisition of property. Micah directs his fire at the unscrupulous landowners who enlarged their boundaries by seizing fields and houses from the poor. He says that at night they plan these evil deeds and then in the morning they carry them out because they have the power to do so. He says, *"They defraud a man of his home,"* which indicates that the rich were using the law to pervert justice, no doubt through bribery. In this way Micah hit at both the landowner and the corrupt system that gave no protection to the poor.

The prophets of Israel, speaking in the name of Yahweh had always hated injustice and oppression. Long before the era of the writing prophets in the eighth century BC, men with prophetic ministries such as Nathan spoke firmly against greed and injustice. After David had arranged for Uriah the Hittite to be killed in battle so that he could take Bathsheba as his wife, Nathan took his own life in his hands and told David a story about a rich man taking a poor man's only lamb. David is said to have *"burned with anger"* against the rich man's injustice, to which Nathan responded, *"You are the man!"* (2 Sam 12:7). He followed this with a pronouncement in the name of Yahweh the God of Israel against injustice.

The earliest of the eighth century prophets, Amos, majored on injustice. His opening pronouncement against Israel was, *"They trample on the heads of the poor as upon the dust of the ground and deny justice to the oppressed"* (Am 2:7). This tradition was continued by Isaiah and Hosea in the same period as well as by Jeremiah and Ezekiel in the sixth century BC. In the view of all the prophets of Israel God hates injustice and oppression.

Isaiah of Jerusalem, who preceded Micah, used almost a whole chapter to pronounce woes and judgement upon injustice. His most famous phrase was, *"Woe to those who call evil good and good evil, who put darkness for light and light for darkness, who put bitter for sweet and sweet for bitter"* (Is 5:20). The theology behind all of Isaiah's condemnation of injustice was that God hates injustice: *"The Lord Almighty will be exalted by his justice, and the holy God will show himself holy by his righteousness"* (Is 5:16).

Micah follows Isaiah in stating, *"Therefore, the Lord says: I am planning disaster against this people, from which you cannot save yourselves."* In the same way as the people of Israel were planning iniquity, God was planning disaster in response. Isaiah had declared that *"the Lord Almighty has a day in store for all the proud and lofty, for all that is exalted"* (Is 2:12). He said that the pride of men would be humbled. Micah declared that a time of calamity would come and people would be reduced to crying out, *"We are utterly ruined."*

Micah could foresee the Assyrian invasion from which there would be no protection because the people had turned their backs upon God and thereby scorned the protection that he would give in accordance with his covenant promises. Micah knew the Assyrians to be a cruel and ruthless people who would show no mercy, but he believed God would allow them to execute judgement upon the people of Israel for their sinfulness in breaking the covenant with Yahweh and worshipping other gods. The Assyrians would thus be instruments in the hands of God.

Micah's final pronouncement in this passage was, *"Therefore you will have no one in the assembly of the Lord to divide the land by lot."* In this he was looking forward to the time when the remnant would return to the land after the exile. The rich who oppress the poor with injustice would not be among the faithful remnant who return. The Assyrians would reassign the fields of those who had obtained them by injustice. In this way the justice of the Lord would be seen.

5 FALSE PROPHETS   Micah 2:6-11

"Do not prophesy," their prophets say. "Do not prophesy about these things, disgrace will not overtake us." Should it be said, O house of Jacob: "Is the Spirit of the Lord angry? Does he do such things?"

This passage shows how the preaching and prophecies of Micah were hitting home at the landowners and the businessmen of Judah. He was told to stop his prophecies of the wrath of God upon the house of Jacob. They hated his preaching. They said that the Lord was not angry with the people of Israel. He would not say such things.

Micah said that his words were good for those who were living upright lives; but he was referring to those businessmen – the *nouveaux riches* – who stripped possessions from anyone, even visiting tradesmen. The unjust businessmen and landowners would stop at nothing to increase their wealth. They had no compassion for the poor, taking over the houses of women and children, driving them into poverty. The lack of law and order and widespread corruption and injustice increased the gap between rich and poor.

Micah was convinced that the sinfulness of the nation, which was causing immense suffering to the powerless, had reached a point when the judgement of God was inevitable. The best advice for the people suffering oppression was *"Get up, go away!"* The whole land was defiled: it was *"ruined, beyond all remedy"* and Micah could foresee no future for Israel.

We do not know whether or not Micah was foreseeing the end of Samaria when the Assyrians invaded in 722 BC and the city was destroyed and the depopulation of the countryside began. Micah does not state clearly whether he was referring to the northern kingdom of Israel or to Judah, his own home territory. In his view they were all the people of Israel, and he saw similar iniquity in all parts of the two kingdoms. Bribery and corruption among the political leaders and in business were common both in Samaria and in Jerusalem.

Micah returned to the subject of 'prophecy' in this passage. He focused upon false prophecy and false teaching which had been known in Israel since the days of the settlement under Joshua. Part of the folk history of the nation featured Balaam and King Balak who wanted him to curse the people of Israel. The story told in Numbers 22 – 24 was of the Israelites entering the plains of Moab and camping along the Jordan near Jericho which engendered fear in King Balak that his nation would be overrun by the Israelites. He employed a renowned 'prophet' to use his powers of divination to bring calamity upon Israel, but to no avail.

In Micah's day the false prophets were active both in Israel and Judah. They were the ones who were particularly active in opposing his mission. They hated anyone who declared the truth because that endangered their own livelihood. They earned their living through giving what in New Testament days would have been known as 'words of knowledge'. In their case these so-called 'prophecies' would have been obtained through divination for which they used all kinds of cultic symbols or household idols.

In this passage we find Micah describing the work of false prophets who were undermining his own ministry by bringing a message of prosperity. Hence Micah declares, *"If a liar and deceiver comes and says, 'I will prophesy for you plenty of wine and beer,' he would be just the prophet for this people!"* There were plenty of so-called 'prophets' in the difficult days when many people were suffering. People were longing for good news of better days, so they were open to deception. If a man or woman claiming to be a prophet came with a personalised message of good fortune, they would gladly pay the fee demanded.

Both Jeremiah and Ezekiel had to deal with false prophets who were giving messages that were contrary to the word of God. Jeremiah wrote about them in a letter to the exiles saying that these men were not declaring the word of the Lord (Jer 29:9). Ezekiel also dealt firmly with the false prophets among the exiles who were undermining his ministry (Ezek 13).

By giving the people so-called 'good news' that there was nothing wrong with the nation they were doing immense harm because God was looking for repentance among his people so that they would turn away from their wicked ways and put their trust totally in him. Then he could give them *"a new heart and a new spirit"* (Ezek 36:26). We had the same problem in Britain when the 'Kansas City prophets' came saying a great revival would break out in October 1990 when God was, in truth, calling for repentance in his church.

6 DELIVERANCE OF THE REMNANT
Micah 2:12-13

I will surely gather all of you, O Jacob; I will surely bring together the remnant of Israel. I will bring them together like sheep in a pen, like a flock in its pasture; the place will throng with people.

This is a genuine piece of good news that Micah felt impelled to bring in order to counterbalance the condemnation of the false prophets that he had just given. He did not want to leave the people with no hope. His words at the beginning of this chapter were prophesying disaster and he was not retracting that. The people had ignored the warnings of prophets for too long. The sinfulness of the nation had reached the point where judgement was inevitable, but God still loved his people and so Micah was looking beyond the judgement to the time of repentance followed by blessing that God would pour out. He sees the enormous energy that would be released when the time of blessing came which would be like cattle being released in the springtime.

My daughter and son-in-law had a hotel in the Austrian Tyrol. It is a beautiful traditional Austrian building in a 'chocolate box' setting about halfway up a mountain with a beautiful background on the edge of a village and surrounded by farmland with the mountaintop rising behind them. Their nearest neighbour was a farmer who had a small amount of grazing land behind their hotel and, as is traditional with all the farms around them, he takes his cows up to the top of the mountain for the summer months and then brings them down again in the autumn.

The cattle remain enclosed in the barn throughout the winter months and then in the spring they are released from their stalls. It is the most amazing sight I have ever witnessed. The strength and furious energy of the cows coming out of the barn is beyond description. They thunder across the meadow in joyous release and if there is a fence or a closed gate ahead of them they simply plunge straight through. Nothing can stop them now that they have been set free from captivity. It is a terrifying sight, and no one would survive if they were standing in the way!

This is the kind of energy that Micah was foreseeing for the remnant of Israel released from slavery at the end of the exile. They will break out of their confinement in the land of the enemy and head for the land of Israel with enormous energy. Isaiah catches a little of this energy as he describes the end of the exile in Babylon. *"The ransomed of the Lord will return. They will enter Zion with singing; everlasting joy will crown their heads. Gladness and joy will overtake them, and sorrow and sighing will flee away"* (Is 51:11).

This is what Micah was prophesying for the people of Israel. It would be God who would redeem Israel as he had done in the past when he brought them out of Egypt. *"I will surely gather all of you, O Jacob. I will surely bring together the remnant of Israel."* The people who survived the exile from both Samaria and Judah would be brought back to the land of Israel. They will be brought together in a unity that they had not known, as in the days of Solomon, before the revolt of Jeroboam plunged the ten tribes of Israel into the sins of idolatry, worshipping a golden calf at Bethel and Dan.

Jeremiah foresaw the day coming when God would bring together the separated and scattered tribes of Israel into a new unity. *"The days are coming, declares the Lord, when I will bring my people Israel and Judah back from captivity"* (Jer 30:3). Jeremiah also foresaw the energy and joy that would accompany their release. *"They will come and shout for joy on the heights of Zion; they will rejoice in the bounty of the Lord"* (Jer 31:12).

Micah goes even farther in foreseeing the regathering of the people of Israel as having messianic significance. He says, *"Their king will pass through before them, the Lord at their head."* Ezekiel, in his vision of the new Jerusalem, prophesied that the temple would be rebuilt after the end of the exile. He said that Jerusalem would have a permanently shut east gate (as it is today) where the glory of the Lord had departed before the Babylonians attacked the city. He said, *"The prince himself is the only one who may sit inside the gateway to eat in the presence of the Lord"* (Ezek 44:3). Ezekiel does not define the 'Prince' as Messiah, but it is significant that he is allowed to sit in the presence of God – an honour that could only be given to Messiah.

7 UNJUST LEADERS AND JUDGES   Micah 3:1-4

Listen, you leaders of Jacob, you rulers of the house of Israel. Should you not know justice, you who hate good and love evil; who tear the skin from my people and the flesh from their bones.

This opening statement is addressed to both Judah (Jacob) and Israel. Micah is referring to the complex system of justice in both kingdoms. The titled 'leaders' and 'rulers' were the men who sat at the gates of the city dealing with small disputes, although they could have been judges in the courts of law dealing with more serious matters. Micah is concerned with all those who deal with issues of justice in the nation because he sees corruption in the whole system and practice of law. He asks an aggressive question – "Should you not know justice?"

Of course, these men who were in positions of leadership in the nation should know justice. Justice was part of the very nature of God and any offence against justice was an offence against God himself. The characteristics of the leaders of the nation were defined by God in an instruction to Moses, *"Choose some wise, understanding and respected men from each of your tribes, and I will set them over you"* (Deut 1:13). Then in 1:17, the standard of justice was set by God, *"Do not show partiality in judging; hear both small and great alike. Do not be afraid of any man, for judgement belongs to God."* If the leaders of the nation had known God, they would have known 'justice'. They would not show favour to anyone in a particular group, neither would they be influenced by bribery or threats from other men.

Sadly, the leaders of the nation did not know justice because they did not know God, and therefore they were leading the nation astray. They were men who turned justice upside down in the same way as they hated good and loved evil. Micah compared these leaders to cannibals – doing the worst possible things that human beings could do to each other. They were tearing the skin off their fellow human beings, breaking their bones and chopping up their bodies like a butcher preparing meat for cooking in a pan.

The terrible things that these leaders were doing were to people who belonged to God. They were his chosen people through whom he intended to reveal himself to the nations. These were the people whom God had rescued from Egypt to whom he had said *"I will take you as my own people, and I will be your God. Then you will know that I am the Lord your God, who brought you out from under the yoke of the Egyptians"* (Ex 6:7).

It is worth looking at the Hebrew here because Micah was conveying a truth that can easily be missed. The term *"people of God"* (*'am YHWH'*) is used many times throughout the Bible, but here in 3:2, Micah speaks of those who *"tear the skin from my people (**ammi**) and the flesh from their bones"*. 'My people' (*ammi*) is the term used for those who are particularly close relatives – kith and kin. It is used by Ruth when speaking to her mother-in-law Naomi. She said, *"Where you go I will go, and where you stay I will stay. Your people will be **my people** and your God my God" (Ruth 1:16)*.

Isaiah used the term in the same way when he declared judgement upon *"those who make unjust laws, to those who issue oppressive decrees, to deprive the poor of their rights and withhold justice from the oppressed of **my people*** (*ammi*, Is 10:1-2). This is particularly important because Micah is here using the term in relation to oppression and injustice that the people were suffering.

Similarly, it is used by Jeremiah in lamentation of the suffering of the people in Babylon: *"O my Comforter in sorrow, my heart is faint within me. Listen to the cry of my people (**ammi**) from a land far away"* (Jer 8:18-19). In the same way in Lamentations, the term 'my people' (*ammi*) is used to refer to the tender love of God for his people who were suffering terrible cruelty at the hands of their oppressors. *"Streams of tears flow from my eyes because **my people** (ammi) are destroyed"* (Lam 3:48).

The final verse in this section pronounces judgement upon the unrighteous. The leaders who turned justice upside down will themselves suffer the kind of injustice they show to others. Isaiah makes a similar pronouncement against those who *"acquit the guilty for a bribe but deny justice to the innocent . . . Therefore, the Lord's anger burns against his people"* (Is 5:23-25). Micah sees a day coming when the unjust rulers will cry out to God for help, but he will hide his face from them.

8 MORE FALSE PROPHECIES   Micah 3:5-8

This is what the Lord says: As for the prophets who lead my people astray, if one feeds them, they proclaim 'peace'; if he does not, they prepare to wage war against him.

In the earliest days of the history of Israel Moses denounced false prophets who misled the people, leading them to rebel against God. They were to be purged from among the people of Israel (Deut 13:1-11). False prophecy is as serious as idolatry. It leads to false teaching which leads people astray. What Micah had seen in Israel was the secularisation of religion. The 40 year reign of Jeroboam II was a period of peace and prosperity, with the country benefitting from increased trade.

A generation of *nouveau riche* emerged who worshipped material things and were greedy for gain, enjoying personal wealth and caring nothing for the poor and the powerless. Micah's description of the prophets is very revealing. If you put food in their mouths, what came out would be nice messages of encouragement and prosperity; but if you did not, they would wage war against you. Religion had become polluted with the values of the world.

The consequences of this false religion would be to bring darkness upon the land in the same way as they turned upside down the true teaching of God. Micah was here echoing the words of his predecessor Isaiah among the eighth century prophets. He had proclaimed woe to those who turned truth upside down – to those who *"call evil good and good evil, who put darkness for light and light for darkness, who put bitter for sweet and sweet for bitter"* (Is 5:20).

In the same way, Micah could foresee judgement coming upon the false prophets who were misleading the people. It is interesting that Micah reverted to the ancient name 'seers' for these 'prophets'. The Prophet Samuel was known as a seer (1 Sam 9:9). A seer was essentially one who prophesied by receiving visions, but visions could be from God or from another source. The Prophet Isaiah was known as a seeing prophet (Is 1:1).

God spoke to Aaron and Miriam on the subject of divine visitations. He said, *"When a prophet of the Lord is among you, I reveal myself in visions, I speak to him in dreams"* (Num 12:6). The essential element here is that the receiver has to be a genuine prophet of the Lord. This was the problem faced by all the prophets who encountered false prophets who usually received their visions by divination, and divination was roundly condemned in the Torah, *"Do not practise divination or sorcery"* (Lev 19:26).

Ezekiel was troubled by false prophets among the exiles in Babylon. He said that they were prophesying out of their own imagination, and *"their visions are false and their divinations a lie"* (Ezek 13:6). Jeremiah had to deal firmly with these same false prophets in Babylon. In his first letter to the exiles he warned, *"Do not let the prophets and diviners among you deceive you. Do not listen to the dreams you encourage them to have"* (Jer 29:8). This is a similar statement to that made in Zech 10:2, *"The idols speak deceit, diviners see visions that lie; they tell dreams that are false, they give comfort in vain,"* which was exactly what Micah was facing back in the eighth century where the false prophecies were popular among the people – the false prophets gave messages that the people loved.

Micah pronounced the sentence of judgement upon the false prophets, *"The seers will be ashamed, and the diviners disgraced,"* they would cover their faces. A covering of the beard was the traditional sign of mourning as when Ezekiel was mourning the death of his wife, and he was told not to show any outward signs of his grief by covering his beard (Ezek 24:17). This was a sign of lament that would be seen among the false prophets according to Micah. They would be grieving for the failure of their prophecies to be fulfilled because God would not answer them.

In the final statement in this section Micah boldly asserts the genuineness of his own prophetic calling: *"as for me, I am filled with power, with the Spirit of the Lord."* His credentials as a genuine prophet sent by God and anointed by the power of God should be evident from the exercise of his calling. His mission was to declare the word of the Lord to the people of Israel: *"to Jacob his transgression and to Israel his sin".*

What was lacking among the people in Micah's day was what would be defined by the Apostle Paul centuries later as the spiritual gift of *"distinguishing between spirits"* (1 Cor 12:10), the ability to perceive the source of a spiritual pronouncement.

9 THE WORD OF THE LORD TO ISRAEL
Micah 3:9-12

Hear this, you leaders of the house of Jacob, you rulers of the house of Israel, who despise justice and distort all that is right, who build Zion with bloodshed, and Jerusalem with wickedness.

Micah followed this declaration with a direct charge against the priests and prophets of Jerusalem. It was the responsibility of the priests to teach the terms of the Covenant and to explain the meaning of the Torah, helping the people to understand the many different aspects of its teaching. There was certainly no tradition in Israel of the priests charging for their services. This teaching of the word of God was part of their responsibilities for which they were set aside and given provisions. It was monstrous that they should be charging for these services. In addition, those who were prophets were telling fortunes – practising divination which was strictly forbidden in the Law (Lev 19:26), and they were charging money from the people.

Micah had already set out charges of injustice against the judges and the rulers of the people so that these sinful practices of the religious leaders compounded with the collective wickedness of all the leaders of the nation, both secular and religious, could be exposed. Despite all this injustice and the exploitation of the people whom they were supposed to serve, these unrighteous leaders added to their sins by boasting that Yahweh the God of Israel was with them. They were actually doing all these evil things in the name of the Lord. It was their confidence that God was with them that gave them a false sense of security, so they were able to dismiss the charges that Micah or anyone else brought against them.

"Is not the Lord amongst us?" they boasted. Therefore, no disaster can befall us! This sense of absolute security among the leaders of the nation in the city of Jerusalem can only be understood in the context of the history of that period. Among all the citizens of Jerusalem there was a sense of superiority that they were in the great city of David which had at its centre the mound of Zion upon which had been built the beautiful temple which was the dwelling of Yahweh

the God of Israel. It was he who had redeemed his people from Egypt and led them through the desert to this place and he had promised that he would watch over his people for their good in all generations. This elevated the leaders to an almost supernatural status in the land of Judah, hence their boast that Yahweh was amongst them and therefore the city was inviolable.

Micah is the last of the eighth century BC prophets who were sent by God specifically with warnings of the disaster threatened by the rising power of the Assyrian Empire. Their message was that only Yahweh the God of Israel had the power to withstand the onslaught. They taught that the covenant pledge of God's protection depended upon the faithfulness of the people in keeping their part of the terms of the covenant – namely that they had no other God than Yahweh.

Amos, Isaiah and Hosea had all given powerful pleas for repentance, for the rejection of idolatry and for total trust in the God of Israel. Their warnings had gone unheeded and in Micah's time disaster was falling upon Samaria. This made the warnings that Micah was bringing to Jerusalem all the more poignant, but the superiority of the leadership in Jerusalem enabled them to scorn this man from Moresheth – who did he think he was? – coming from some little country town to the great city of Jerusalem? They certainly had no reason to heed the ramblings of a country bumpkin.

Nevertheless, Micah's dramatic description of the future of Jerusalem made an indelible impression. He said that Jerusalem would become a heap of rubble, and the temple mount would be overgrown with thickets. This terrible threat became so memorable that it was remembered, word for word, for more than a century. It was when Jeremiah was facing a trial for his life 100 years later that some of the elders in Jerusalem related the exact words of Micah (Jer 26:18). They were said to have been given during the reign of Hezekiah and we know from Isaiah 37:14 that both the king and the prophet went into the temple and spread the issue before the Lord, with the result that a plague swept through the Assyrian army and Jerusalem was saved.

Micah's vivid description of the destruction of Jerusalem together with the ministry of Isaiah delayed the judgement upon Jerusalem. Sadly, there was no repentance and trust in God to change the nation, and in 586 BC Micah's prophecy of the destruction of Jerusalem was fulfilled by the Babylonians.

10 THE MOUNTAIN OF THE LORD   Micah 4:1-5

In the last days the mountain of the Lord's people will be established as chief among the mountains; it will be raised above the hills, and peoples will stream to it. Many nations will come and say, "Come, let us go up to the mountain of the Lord, to the house of the God of Jacob."

This is one of the best loved pieces in the Bible. It beautifully expresses the hope of all human beings who would love to live in a world where there is peace and security; where there is no fear, and all people live together in righteousness and mutual respect. The passage is repeated almost word for word as in Isaiah 2 where it precedes a powerful warning that the day will come when God will deal with the arrogance of human beings. Here, in Micah's ministry, it is set immediately after the most devastating pronouncement of judgement upon Jerusalem. The prophet turns from the scene of destruction and heaps of rubble to God's ultimate purpose for the city that bears his name.

Both Jewish and Christian scholars have debated for centuries whether Isaiah or Micah wrote these words, but no one really knows. They both ministered in the same period although Isaiah preceded Micah, possibly by some 30 or 40 years. Another possibility is that these words came from an entirely different source to which they both had access, but clearly, they both saw them as coming from God.

The mountain of the Lord is the Temple Mount in Jerusalem whose status will be raised high above all the high places of the world with their altars for the worship of idols. This will attract people from all nations who will stream to Jerusalem to worship at the temple. This word 'stream' is a strange verb to use as it literally means streaming along water in the same way as people in boats streamed down a fast-flowing river, but it is descriptive of a fast flow of people in a great hurry – showing the eagerness of the people to get to Jerusalem! They say to each other, *"Come, let us go up to the house of Yahweh the God of Israel."* He would teach them the true way of life so that they could walk under his direction.

The Torah, the righteous teaching of God will go out from Zion enabling all peoples to walk in the way of the Lord. God will act as a righteous judge and settle disputes between people which will remove the necessity and the desire to go to war, because he will judge rightly. This is in strong contrast to the corrupt judges Micah has just been describing who were leaders of the people of Israel. These corrupt judges accepted bribes and allowed the rich to seize the property of the poor and powerless, while the religious leaders, priests and prophets, distorted the word of God for their own enrichment.

Micah foresaw the day coming when the true teaching of God would prevail in the land of Israel and then people throughout the world will recognise the value of God's truth coming from the temple of Yahweh, the God of Israel, and they will be eager to go to hear his word and to receive his teaching and learn his ways that will enable them to walk in his paths. The two words used here – 'ways' and 'paths' – symbolise the truth at the heart of God's creation of humanity that he intended them to follow for their own well-being, happiness, and fulfilment.

God's ways and paths through life were being distorted by human sin, but the day would come when the truth would go out from Zion and be recognised by all people and the nations would stream to Jerusalem to receive the truth and learn to walk in the ways of the Lord, the one true God and Lord of all creation who, in Isaiah's words, held the nations in his hands *"like a drop in a bucket"* (Is 40:15).

Instead of fighting, people will beat their swords into ploughshares – transforming implements of war intended for taking life, into implements for producing life by feeding people. All the nations will be at peace with each other, and they will no longer train armies to fight because they will be walking in the ways of truth and righteousness, following the ways of the Lord. In that day everyone will sit under their own vine or fig tree without fear because there will be mutual respect. Each one will honour other people and respect their rights so that no one will live in fear of robbers or unjust rulers. Even those who go to Jerusalem still walking in the ways of their own gods, will walk in the way of the Lord God of Israel.

11 THE WAY OF THE LORD   Micah 4:6-10

"In that day," declares the Lord, "I will gather the lame; I will assemble the exiles and those I have brought to grief. I will make the lame a remnant, those driven away a strong nation. The Lord will rule over them in Mount Zion from that day and for ever."

The last section with its vision of peace and security, concluded with the declaration, *"The Lord Almighty has spoken"* (4:4), guaranteeing that the vision would one day be fulfilled. In this section God sets out his plan for how he intends working out his purposes. It is of great significance because it reveals something of the nature of God which can be seen through his ways.

Instead of assessing the power and strength of the resources at his disposal for carrying out his plans, God declares, *"I will gather the lame; I will assemble the exiles and those I have brought to grief."* This is a wonderful example of what may be described as the 'scandal of God's justice' that turns upside down the values of the world. He is not looking for those to whom the world ascribes power and glory – the rich and powerful. He takes those with no status, the outcasts of society and those who lack physical strength. They are the favoured ones whom God redeems and transforms and empowers for the accomplishment of his purposes.

There are many examples of this in Scripture. King David is always regarded as the ideal king, but he started as a lad facing the giant Goliath armed with a bag of pebbles and immense trust in God. David followed the same principle in his leadership. When he was on the run from both Saul and from the Philistines, he established a base at the Cave of Adullam where *"all those who were in distress or in debt or discontented gathered round him, and he became their leader"* (1 Sam 22:2). It was this ragged remnant that David trained to be a powerful army of warriors who conquered Jerusalem, which was said to be impregnable and set it up as the capital of Israel.

Micah saw God employing the same principle of using the most unlikely people to fulfil his purposes. Indeed, this principle was ingrained into the history of Israel where God had responded to the cries of an enslaved and powerless minority in Egypt. He had brought them out into the desert where he had welded them into a nation with a purpose – that purpose was for God to reveal himself to the world through them. As Moses had said, *"The Lord did not set his affection on you and choose you because you were more numerous than other peoples, for you were the fewest of all peoples. But it was because the Lord loved you"* (Deut 7:7-8).

Micah was given an amazing insight to God's ways that led to him foreseeing how God was going to fulfil his purposes for Israel that were central to his redemptive purposes for humanity. It was all here packed into these few verses with the promise that through the agony of what is going to happen to them, the end result would be a triumph for the grace of God who would redeem his people, transforming disaster into glorious redemption.

These verses can only be understood against the background of the history of the time when Micah was speaking. The good King Hezekiah who, together with Isaiah had seen a powerful move of God in saving Jerusalem from conquest by the Assyrians (Is 37:36-38), had recently died and been succeeded by his son Manasseh who became a byword for evil in the history of Israel. It was he who rebuilt the high places his father Hezekiah had destroyed, brought idolatry into the temple, and filled Jerusalem with blood (2 Kgs 21:3-16). People were crying out for a righteous king and Micah reassures them that the day will come when righteous kingship will *"come to the Daughter of Jerusalem."*

Before that promise would be fulfilled Micah foresaw Jerusalem writhing in agony, but he saw that it would become the birth pangs of a new creation. *"You will go to Babylon; there you will be rescued. There the Lord will redeem you."*

It is in Babylon that Micah foresaw God redeeming Israel by using a remnant whom he would rescue from enslavement. This action of rescuing or redeeming (Hebrew *ga'al)* his people in Babylon is highly significant. The verb *ga'al* can also be used in a legal sense for regaining something that was lost as in Leviticus 25:49. Jeremiah uses a similar word *padah* when he says, *"For the Lord will ransom Jacob and redeem them"* (Jer 31:11). God loves to achieve his purposes through the most unlikely people. He is the Lord of redemption!

12 THE WAY TO REDEMPTION   Micah 4:11 – 5:1

But now many nations are gathered against you. They say, "Let her be defiled, let our eyes gloat over Zion!" But they do not know the thoughts of the Lord; they do not understand his plan, he who gathers them like sheaves to the threshing floor.

In this passage Micah turns away from his prophesying the future to what was happening that day in his lifetime. He looked around and saw the gathering storm that he had been predicting. The first signs of the disaster that he had been describing, were now to be seen. The nations were gathering against Israel. There was an increasing movement among the nations in hostility against Israel. The hostile nations are not named, but they are said to be many in number and their hatred of Israel is described as seeking to defile Jerusalem.

This sounds like the sentiments expressed in Psalm 83:4 where many nations were conspiring together against the people of Israel; *"Come," they say, "let us destroy them as a nation, that the name of Israel be remembered no more."* The Psalmist continued describing the widespread movement among the nations who were planning a co-ordinated attack to completely destroy the nation of Israel, which is similar to the intentions of Nazi Germany in the 1930s; and similar to the policy of Hamas at the time of their attack upon Israel October 2023. The anti-Semitic chanting, "From the River to the Sea" in many Western nations was a sign of the widespread desire to wipe Israel off the map of the world. That has been a desire among many nations throughout history since the eighth century BC or even before.

Micah could see the hatred among the nations directed towards Zion, the holy place of the God of Israel. Jerusalem with its great temple built by Solomon was already widely recognised as a holy place that was causing a rising level of jealousy among the nations. Israel was seen as special to God and human beings all want to control God. Micah says they gloated over Zion: *"But they do not know the thoughts of the Lord; they do not understand his plan."* This statement is very similar to the statement in Isaiah, *"For my thoughts are not your thoughts, neither are your ways my ways," declares the Lord. "As the heavens are higher than the earth, so are my ways higher than your ways and my thoughts than your thoughts"* (Is 55:8-9).

This is the tragedy of humanity; human beings fail to understand God, and therefore do not understand his plans. Micah's words are as valid today as they were in the eighth century BC when they were spoken. The Gentile nations were vaguely aware that Jerusalem was special to God and that the people of Israel were different from the Gentile nations, but they did not understand the God of Israel, or his nature and purposes. This generated suspicion, jealousy, and an overwhelming desire to seize control.

This desire for power and control had been active from the beginning of creation. It was the human objective to be like God – to seize his power, to take control of the universe. This was the motivation of the nations and their hatred of Israel that Micah was perceiving. They simply did not understand the God of Israel who would not allow them to destroy his covenant people. He would gather them together *"like sheaves to the threshing floor"* where they would be slaughtered.

This is very similar to the vision given to Ezekiel in chapters 38 and 39. Ezekiel foresaw the worldwide hatred of the people of Israel reaching such a point that the existence of Israel is threatened. At that point when Israel is powerless to defend itself, according to the vision described by Ezekiel, God would act on behalf of his people. This is the scenario of Ezekiel 39 when the hatred of Israel – which in essence is hatred of God – threatens the whole of humanity, so God intervenes to destroy those who are implacably opposed to truth and righteousness.

God has preserved the Jews over the past 3000 years, but neither Israel nor the Gentile nations have understood the nature and purposes of God which have been clearly revealed through the prophets God raised up during the eighth to the sixth centuries BC. Jeremiah's 'Temple Sermon' (Jer 7) summarised the things God hates such as injustice, oppression, the misuse of power, violence, bloodshed and war, lies, deceit, faithlessness, idolatry, adultery and sexual aberrations. There is therefore no reason why humanity should be in ignorance of the ways of God. This is why, in the closing days of Hezekiah's reign, Micah sees the Assyrian troops striking the king on his cheek, but in the future God would give his people power to overcome their enemies.

13 THE HONOURING OF BETHLEHEM
Micah 5:2-5

But you, Bethlehem Ephrathah, though you are small among the clans of Judah, out of you will come for me one who will be ruler over Israel.

This is a beautiful messianic oracle fully in line with the nature and values of God which were revealed in 4:6 where it was said that it was God's intention to work out his purposes through the most unlikely people; the oppressed, the exiles and the remnant. God loves to choose those whom the world despises and to use them in the work of the kingdom. This teaching is also to be found in the words of Jesus and especially in his parables, such as the tiny mustard seed that becomes a great tree, and the young man who wasted his inheritance but was nevertheless greatly honoured when he repented and returned.

Here, Micah prophesied that a great ruler would come from the little village of Bethlehem, which was the area where King David spent his boyhood tending sheep on his family land. Micah hears God saying that although Bethlehem is small and insignificant, *"out of you will come for me one who will be a ruler over Israel."* It is the phrase *"for me"* that is particularly significant in the history of Bethlehem.

When God sent the Prophet Samuel to the family of Jesse, he said *"I have chosen one of his sons to be king"* (1 Sam 16:1). Samuel then had to find which of the sons God had chosen. God does not do for us things that we can do ourselves in the gifting that he has given us. Samuel had the gift of discernment which he exercised in discovering David, who was God's anointed leader. Micah does not identify the anointed leader because it would not be in his lifetime, but the people of Israel, or at least their leaders, should have been able to identify Messiah when he was sent. Sadly, as John says, he came to his own people *"but his own did not receive him"* (Jn 1:11).

Micah appears to foresee the rejection of the anointed one by the people. He says, *"Therefore Israel will be abandoned"* – there will be a time of desolation for Israel. Jeremiah also foresaw a time when God would lift his cover of protection due to the gross sins of the people and their leaders. He wept at what he foresaw coming: *"Oh, that my head were a spring of water and my eyes a fountain of tears! I would weep day and night for the slain of my people"* (Jer 9:1). And Hosea heard God grieving, *"How can I give you up Ephraim? How can I hand you over, Israel?"* (Hos 11:8).

The sins of the people were so great that God would not protect them for ever. In the time of King Zedekiah when he broke the promise of allegiance that he had given to Nebuchadnezzar in the name of Yahweh God of Israel, God *"thrust them from his presence"* (2 Kings 24:20). The destruction of Jerusalem in 586 BC and the widespread devastation of the land of Judah brought a time of desolation. It is recorded in Lamentations, *"The Lord has done what he planned; he has fulfilled his word, which he decreed long ago. He has overthrown you without pity, he has let the enemy gloat over you"* (Lam 2:17).

The time of desolation would end when the Lord brought the remnant of the exiles back from Babylon which would be like the rebirth of the nation after the full term of gestation, like a woman reaching the time of her labour. In the same way, and at the right time, God would send his Messiah, born in Bethlehem. To describe this momentous event Micah returns to the metaphor of David, the shepherd boy whom God raised up to lead his people righteously. Micah sees Messiah as a good shepherd caring for his sheep, ensuring that they are fed and watered and guarded against danger. Through his majesty and strength, the people would live in peace and security.

Ezekiel did more than anyone else to prepare the faithful remnant of believers to return to the land, to rebuild Jerusalem in preparation for the age of Messiah. It is possible that Micah not only foresaw the end of the exile in Babylon and the return of the people as prophesied, but it is also possible that Micah was foreseeing the long period of desolation for Israel in being removed from the land by the Romans who destroyed Jerusalem in 135 AD, renaming Judah and Samaria 'Palestine' – 'land of the Philistines' – as a deliberate insult to the Jews. The rebirth of Israel in 1948 may also be what Micah was foreseeing.

14 THE ASSYRIAN INVASION   Micah 5:5-9

When the Assyrian invades our land and marches through our fortresses, we will raise against him seven shepherds, even eight leaders of men. They will rule the land of Assyria with the sword, the land of Nimrod with drawn sword.

This is a difficult passage to translate and even more difficult to understand. All biblical scholars struggle to interpret its meaning which results in a wide spectrum of views, with liberal scholars even dismissing it as being the work of later generations rather than of Micah. The view we are taking here is that there is a continuity running right through the book of Micah and that the messianic mission of Israel that Micah unfolds at the beginning of chapter 5 which was expounded in the previous section, is the central focus of Micah's work.

The five verses that we are now considering can only be understood in the context of the previous verses of the Messiah coming out of Bethlehem. When the expected Assyrian invasion happens, it will not take God by surprise and it will all be part of his will and purpose. Israel is a sinful nation full of idolatry and a lack of faith in the God of their fathers, but God uses sinful nations like Assyria and Babylon – the land of Nimrod – in the working out of his purposes. God will raise up seven or eight righteous men who will be given divine power to reverse the onslaught of the enemy and even to exercise influence over Nineveh and Babylon.

This will not happen immediately, but it will be the postexilic remnant who will exercise a transformative influence, not only in Israel but throughout the region that includes all the surrounding Gentile nations. This will be a fulfilment of the messianic vision that Micah expressed in verse 4, *"He will stand and shepherd his flock in the strength of the Lord, in the majesty of the name of the Lord his God."* What Micah was foreseeing was what Ezekiel foresaw more than a century later in Babylon, that God was preparing a faithful remnant of believers whom he would use to rebuild Jerusalem in preparation for the messianic age.

Micah was already looking ahead to that time and he saw the small settlements of Israelites in the exile in the Assyrian and Babylonian Empires as already exercising a messianic influence. He says, *"The remnant of Jacob will be among the nations"* and their presence there will be like showers of rain falling on dry grass that waters the land and makes it fruitful. Although they are living in enemy territory the faithful remnant will exercise an amazing influence that will actually bring blessing and prosperity for those among whom they are living. This is very much in line with what Jeremiah was foreseeing when he wrote his first letter to the exiles who were bemoaning their misfortune and weeping beside the rivers of Babylon.

Jeremiah wrote, *"Seek the peace and prosperity of the city to which I have carried you into exile"* (Jer 29:7). That would have been extremely difficult for the exiles, and the next word was even more difficult when he told them to pray to the Lord for Babylon! Jeremiah said, *"Pray to the Lord for it, because if it prospers, you too will prosper. Yes this is what the Lord Almighty, the God of Israel says: 'Do not let the prophets and diviners among you deceive . . . They are prophesying lies to you in my name.'"*

Jeremiah then declared that God had good plans for his people for the future, which was very much in line with his own ministry, a ministry of both 'uprooting and tearing down' as well as building up (Jer 31:28). Micah foresees all this in a brilliant passage where he says that the remnant of Israel will be among the Gentile nations *"like a lion among the beasts of the forest, like a young lion among the flock of sheep, which mauls and mangles as it goes."*

This would have sounded very strange to those who heard Micah, but God would use them to attack corruption and injustice to bring righteousness, peace, and prosperity. So the faithful remnant would actually triumph over their enemies in quite an amazing way that would turn upside down the plans of the enemy who came to invade Israel, to murder and destroy. God had good plans for his own people, and he would use them to overturn the plans of the enemy and actually bring peace and prosperity to their land which was the whole purpose of the messianic age. A small foretaste of this age of peace and prosperity would already be seen through the influence of the faithful remnant of believers among the Gentile nations until the time of the second coming of Jesus the Messiah.

15 THE COMING DAY OF THE LORD
Micah 5:10-15

"In that day," declares the Lord, "I will destroy your horses from among you and demolish your chariots. I will destroy the cities of your land and tear down all your strongholds."

Micah recognised that the righteousness of God would inevitably lead to a day of recompense when God would deal with the sinfulness of his people whom he had chosen to reveal himself to the Gentile nations. The eighth century prophets who preceded Micah all foresaw such times of judgement. Amos began his ministry with strong declarations against the two nations of Judah and Israel (Am 2:4-8). Isaiah saw a day coming when God would deal with all the proud and lofty, when human pride would be humbled, and God alone would be exalted (Is 2:12-21). Hosea foresaw a time when God would send fire upon the cities of Judah (Hos 8:14) and days of punishment upon Israel (Hos 9:7).

Micah saw four reasons why God should send a day of judgement upon the people of Israel. He is most likely in this passage to be referring to his own people of Judah, as the Assyrian invasion of Samaria in 722 BC is thought by most biblical scholars to have taken place during the time of Micah's ministry or slightly before. The four outstanding sins of Judah that Micah identified were all related to unfaithfulness towards God. They were, trust in military power, trust in fortifications, divination, and idolatry.

The first threat from God was that he would destroy their horses and chariots. This was primarily directed towards what had happened in Lachish since the time of its fortification by Rehoboam. It was the central city of the area known as the Shephelah which included Micah's own hometown of Moresheth. Micah would have known it well and he would often have seen the military parades of horse-drawn chariots which had been purchased from Egypt. He saw this as particularly offensive to God because it was specifically ignoring what God had forbidden when they entered the land of Israel. When they appointed a king, he must not *"acquire great numbers of horses for himself or make the people return to Egypt to get more of them"* (Deut 17:16).

During Micah's lifetime, and for the previous generation both in Judah and Israel, the economy had been prospering with the growth of industry and the development of towns and cities through the increasing wealth of a new middle-class of merchants and homeowners. With increasing wealth, the desire to preserve and protect it led to the fortification of cities. Micah sees this fortification as a lack of trust in God and so he believes that God will tear down their strongholds so that they are forced to put their trust in him alone.

The third sin that Micah foresaw which would bring judgement upon the nation was sorcery and divination. Witchcraft was always deeply offensive to God. The Torah specifically forbade witchcraft; *"Let no-one be found among you who sacrifices his son or daughter in the fire, who practises divination or sorcery, interprets omens, engages in witchcraft, or casts spells, or who is a medium or spiritist or who consults the dead"* (Deut 18:10-11). Sorcery was one of the sins of Babylon that Isaiah roundly condemned. It was one of the ways in which human beings tried to communicate with God, but all the prophets recognised the danger to the people of Israel if they began copying the practices of the Gentiles.

The fourth of the sins of Judah that Micah condemned was idolatry, and in some cities and high places they even displayed Asherah poles. Asherah was a female goddess linked with fertility rites and cultic prostitution that were deeply offensive to God and roundly condemned by all the prophets from the time of Moses who said, *"Do not set up any wooden Asherah pole beside the altar you build to the Lord your God"* (Deut16:21). This word was followed by the statement, *"Do not erect a sacred stone, for these the Lord your God hates."* But sacred stones were part of the foundations of Samaria that had been built by Ahab. Hence the fierceness of the words Micah attributes to God: *"I will uproot from among you your Asherah poles and demolish your cities."*

Micah's final word in this section, is the statement that God will take *"vengeance in anger and wrath upon the nations that have not obeyed me."* This could be referring to Israel and Judah, but the construction of the Hebrew text in the masculine singular points to all nations, as in *"the Lord of all the earth"* (4:13), meaning that the word of the Lord from Jerusalem by which they will be judged should be **heeded by all nations!**

16 THE CASE AGAINST ISRAEL   Micah 6:1-5

Listen to what the Lord says: "Stand up, plead your case before the mountains; let the hills hear what you have to say. Hear, O mountains, the Lord's accusation; listen, you everlasting foundations of the earth."

Each of the writing prophets in the Old Testament, from Amos in the eighth century BC through to Malachi in the fifth century BC, add something to our understanding of the nature and purposes of God. In these five verses Micah envisages God calling a global assembly to witness the grave offence against justice that has been committed by his people Israel. As the God of Creation, he calls the mountains of Israel as witnesses in his accusation against his people who are also part of his creation.

This is not unusual among the prophets. In a magnificent passage, Isaiah sees God enthroned above the circle of the earth while his people are mere grasshoppers. He is not merely the Creator of the physical universe, but he is also Lord of history, holding the nations in his hands as *"a drop in a bucket"*. He calls upon the whole of creation to witness his incomparable majesty and, looking at the night sky he asks, "*Who is my equal? . . . Who created all these?*" (Is 40:12-26).

In a similar mode Jeremiah was astonished and dismayed that Israel had exchanged their God for worthless idols. He called upon the heavens to witness this incredible debacle, *"Be appalled at this, O heavens, and shudder with great horror, declares the Lord"* (Jer 2:12).

Micah uses this celestial law court to witness the incredible injustice that the people of Israel have committed towards the God of Creation who so graciously entered into a covenant relationship with the people of Israel at Mount Sinai. He chose them from among all the families of the earth as the group of human beings through whom he would reveal himself to the nations of the world. His nature, his truth, his justice, and his purposes for humankind, would all be revealed through the history of the people of Israel and their relationship with God. *"Now if you obey me fully and keep my covenant, then out of all nations you will be my treasured possession"* (Ex 19:5).

In verse 3 Micah switches from the formality of a law court where God was lodging a case against his people; he suddenly turns to making a direct appeal to them. The phrase *"My people"*, as we have noted earlier, is of special significance in denoting a close and unique relationship. The question, *"What have I done to you? How have I burdened you?"* is highly significant. The two questions are a mixture of accusation and grief. They are different from the type of formal case presented in a court of law. The questions are more suited to the dispute in an intimate personal relationship between two people who are greatly in love, but one of them is feeling deeply wounded by what the other has done. It is the sort of question that would occur in a marriage if one party had broken their marriage covenant by entering an intimate relationship with another person. This is the grief that God was expressing: *"How could you treat me in this way? What have I done to offend you?"*

The next two verses reiterate some of the saving acts of God, beginning with the way he delivered them from slavery in Egypt. He names the people whom God used who are now a hallowed part of the history of Israel. This is where Micah brings a unique revelation of the nature and purposes of God that is of immense value. In the same way as Hosea saw the wrath of God as a mixture of outraged justice and forgiving love – Micah now adds to our knowledge of God by showing his 'justice' in terms of 'redemption' and in dealing with deception, which is all part of the righteousness of God. It shows God's determination to remain 'just' in his relationship with Israel despite their sinfulness. His purpose is to demonstrate his nature to the nations by revealing himself in the way that he deals with his people who are in a love relationship with him.

The people are called upon to remember – to remember their history! Remember what God had done throughout the journey from Egypt to Canaan. Remember the miracles of provision and how God defended them when they were faced with annihilation by the Moabites. Remember what happened between Shittim and Gilgal on either side of the swollen Jordan River which they all crossed as on dry land. If God could do these things for their forebears, he could certainly do them now! This strengthened their faith and provided a witness to the world.

17 THE REQUIREMENTS OF THE LORD
Micah 6:6-8

With what shall I come before the Lord and bow down before the exalted God? Shall I come before him with burnt offerings . . . He has showed you, O man, what is good . . . to act justly to lovce mercy, and to walk humbly with your God.

These three verses are well known and well loved. They present a theological statement of fundamental importance for an understanding of the relationship between human beings and God. They define the atonement for which human beings constantly seek – how can sinful human beings be reconciled to a holy and righteous God?

Micah had already set out the case against the people of Israel who had undoubtedly broken the covenant relationship with God, the penalties of which were fixed at Mount Sinai and made explicit by Moses. There can be no excuse for the people – the consequences of breaking the covenant by idolatry and unfaithfulness had been made clear by Moses who said that if they became corrupt and practised idolatry they would be destroyed. He said, *"The Lord will scatter you among the peoples, and only a few of you will survive"* (Deut 4:27). Micah could see that God was righteous and just in removing his cover of protection from over the nation and allowing the enemy to bring destruction and death. Hence a generation later Jeremiah could refer to Nebuchadnezzar as the 'servant of God' whom all nations should serve (Jer 27:6-7).

The God of Israel, revealed by the prophets, was also a loving and forgiving God who wanted to bless his people and surround them with peace and prosperity. So the question posed by Micah, *"With what shall I come before the Lord"* in order to be reconciled to him is of fundamental importance. The answers that Micah offers are an indication of how far the nation had drifted away from a right relationship with God and an understanding of his true nature and purposes.

The suggestion of coming to God with offerings of thousands of animals and rivers of oil as a means of doing a deal with God was clearly fantastic! But that was the kind of mentality that Micah saw among the leaders in the nation who thought that their wealth and power enabled them to achieve everything. That was the way they governed the nation, and it symbolised their relationship with God. If God was offended by their behaviour, they could buy him off! In all their human relationships there was a price to be paid – everyone had a price – which they could meet! They were even prepared to pay the ultimate price of sacrificing their most precious possession, their firstborn son, sacrificing the fruit of their body for the sins of their soul – after all, that was what God had required of Abraham although he did not actually enforce it.

The question Micah was confronting was one that all the prophets had faced. Samuel set the standard for Saul: *"To obey is better than sacrifice, and to heed is better than the fat of rams"* (1 Sam 15:22). This was followed some 200 years later by Amos who said that God hated religious feasts and burnt offerings but wanted to see *"justice roll on like a river, righteousness like a never-failing stream"* (Am 5:21-24).

In a similar mode God said to Isaiah, *"I have no pleasure in the blood of bulls and lambs and goats"* (Is 1:11). Yet Solomon, at the dedication of the temple, offered a sacrifice to the Lord of 22,000 cattle and 120,000 sheep and goats (1 Kings 8:63). However, this was a fellowship offering for all the people to eat in thanksgiving, not an atonement for sin. This did not contradict the message of Hosea who heard God saying, *"I desire mercy, not sacrifice"* (Hos 6:6).

This led Micah to declare what God ***does*** require – **he requires nothing! There is nothing we can do to justify ourselves in the eyes of God.** He does not require any human offerings. What he does require is his people to be in a right relationship with him – **to act justly.** The Hebrew word *mishpat* – 'justice' – means living in a right relationship with God and other people, upholding truth, loyalty, integrity, faithfulness, love, and mercy, all of which are part of God's nature. When anyone is walking humbly before God these are the characteristics that will be seen in their life.

This is the central truth of right relationships with God and with our fellow human beings. It all starts with walking humbly and thankfully before God – recognising our human weaknesses and our total dependence upon God to supply all our needs and to direct us in his ways, singing, *"all I have needed thy hand has provided . . ."*

18 ISRAEL'S GUILT AND PUNISHMENT
Micah 6:9-16

Listen! The Lord is calling to the city – and to fear your name is wisdom – Heed the rod and the One who appointed it. Am I still to forget, O wicked house, your ill-gotten treasures and the short ephah, which is accursed?

In these verses Micah builds upon the teaching he has given on atonement – how we can be in a right relationship with God, not through offerings or sacrifices, but by walking humbly in the ways of the Lord. He turns now to look at the reality of the situation in the nation. This needs to be seen against the historical background of the day. Disaster had already fallen upon the northern kingdom of Israel through the invasion of Samaria by the Assyrians. Now there was a new danger threatening Jerusalem and the land of Judah which was coming from the rising power of Babylon. Micah realises that the same judgement that God has allowed to happen to their brothers and sisters in Samaria could happen here in Jerusalem.

Verse 9 begins with a shout of instruction to listen! It is Yahweh who is calling to his people in the city and this appeal to wisdom is more than just exercising common sense – it has a broader meaning of 'wholeness' and 'well-being'. The future existence of the city is threatened with judgement. In the next verse God appeals to all the citizens of Jerusalem, the ordinary people, as well as their leaders. He begins with the practices of merchants in the marketplace where there is open dishonesty among traders using dishonest scales and false weights for measuring the goods they were selling.

This cheating of poor housewives struggling to feed their families was symbolic of the lack of honesty in the nation. It was through dishonesty that the rich had become rich. They had made their fortunes deceitfully by adding violent coercion to deceitful practices in business. The different ways of cheating are described in verse 10 where short measurements, dishonest scales and false weights are used.

These practices are specifically forbidden in the Torah. "*Do not have two differing weights in your bag – one heavy, and one light. Do not have two differing measures in your house – one large, one small. You must have accurate and honest weights and measures, so that you may live long in the land the Lord your God is giving you. For the Lord your God detests anyone who does these things, anyone who deals dishonestly"* (Deut 25:13-16).

The fact that *'living long in the land'* is linked with this prohibition on dishonesty is very significant. It adds powerfully to Micah's warning, and it leads into the specific promise of judgement, *"I have begun to destroy you, to ruin you because of your sins."* The threat of judgement is intensified by the warnings of famine. Their farms would be taken over and what they had planted would be eaten by others. These were all the things that were actually happening to their brothers and sisters in Samaria, and this is what they can expect to happen to them unless there is repentance and change of direction – to walk humbly in the ways of the Lord.

Their sins were not just on the commercial level of dishonesty and corruption, but there was a much more serious charge that the people of Jerusalem and Judah had actually been following the practices of the kings of Israel, Omri and Ahab. This is a terrible charge because these were two of the most wicked kings who followed the ways of Jeroboam who had told the people of Israel not to bother to go up to Jerusalem but to worship the golden bulls he had established at Bethel and Dan.

Omri built Samaria as the capital of Israel and installed sacred stones as part of its foundations, and according to 1 Kings 16:25 *"Omri did evil in the eyes of the Lord and sinned more than all those before him."* His son, Ahab, also did evil in the eyes of the Lord. He, like his father, was heavily into idolatry and actually constructed a temple in Samaria dedicated to Baal. He also established a sex cult in the city with an Asherah pole. As if that were not enough to anger God, Ahab married Jezebel, the daughter of the king of Sidon who brought with her a company of priests of Baal and encouraged all the people of Israel to practise idolatry which led to the conflict on Mount Carmel with the Prophet Elijah. Micah's charge that the people of Jerusalem were doing the same things as Omri and Ahab would undoubtedly have shocked Jerusalem. Micah followed that charge with a prophecy that the destruction of the city would bring scorn and derision from the Gentile nations.

19 ISRAEL'S MISERY   Micah 7:1-7

What misery is mine! I am like one who gathers summer fruit at the gleaning of the vineyard; there is no cluster of grapes to eat, none of the early figs that I crave. The godly have been swept from the land.

In this passage Micah reviews the state of the nation. He had just made the devastating pronouncement that in the city of Jerusalem the people and their leaders were practising all the wicked things that had been done by the worst kings of Israel – the northern kingdom of their brothers and sisters who had broken away from Judah in the time of Rehoboam and Jeroboam. He expresses here his utter misery which is like a poor man going to a vineyard at the end of the harvest looking for anything that had been left. It was explicitly stated in the Torah that farmers were not allowed to go back a second time at the end of harvest. They were to leave their land for the poor to glean anything missed. *"Do not go over your vineyard a second time or pick up the grapes that have fallen. Leave them for the poor and the alien. I am the Lord your God"* (Lev 19:10).

God was continually reminding the Israelites that they themselves were in slavery at one time in their history and he had rescued them. From this they should learn something about the nature and purposes of God, and they should care for the alien and the poor, for this was all part of the justice of God. This comes back into Micah's mind as he reviews the nation. It appears to him that *"the godly have been swept from the land, not one upright man remains."* All that he sees around him are violent men pursuing their own self-interest.

Verse 3 summarises what Micah saw around him in the city of Jerusalem which should have been the city of peace and shalom. It was full of disorder and fear, because *"all men lie in wait to shed blood."* Lawlessness faced all those who walked its streets and the problems began at the very top of society. Judges accepted bribes and those who held political power did what they pleased. The leading citizens were men of violence who conspired together to do whatever they wished. They even cheated their own brothers.

Corruption ran right through society at all levels. At the top, the leaders were a law unto themselves, so every small official or tradesman expected his reward for any service rendered.

Micah felt utterly miserable. He felt completely alone and isolated. He had nothing in common with the people around him. He was heartbroken over what he saw in Jerusalem. He believed that the day of judgement had now come for God to hold his people to account. He said, *"The day of your watchmen has come, the day God visits you."* Every city had watchmen who patrolled the city walls looking to discern any danger for which they must give a warning. In a similar way it was the task of the prophets of Israel to discern spiritual danger and to blow a trumpet of warning. Micah had been giving warnings to the nation for many years and now he had reached the end of the line in what he saw around him.

He saw not merely the bad behaviour of some people. That was simply the outward appearance – the evidence of something much deeper. What he saw was much more fundamental. It was the corruption of the whole civic structure and organisation, the evidence of which could be seen in the lives of the people from top to bottom of society. He had seen corruption among the leaders of the nation, but what he was now looking at was even more significant – no one could be trusted in their relationships. Micah shows great insight in his analysis of the sickness of society. He observes three different levels of relationships starting with friendships among neighbours, then with children, and finally marriage – the ultimate.

It is bad when you cannot trust a friend, when you feel deceived by a neighbour. It is even worse when you are let down by your own son or by a daughter or daughter-in-law. But the ultimate betrayal is when a man finds his wife has been deceiving him or a woman finds her husband has betrayed her. Marriage is a sacred relationship established by God and any offence against the covenant of marriage is a sin against God. It is also fundamental for the health and well-being of society. Widespread marriage breakdown affects the stability of the nation because marriage is one of the pillars in the structure of society. It indicates corruption in the values of the nation and indicates the onset of social dysfunction and national disaster.

20 THE HOPE OF THE NATION Micah 7:7-9

But as for me, I watch in hope for the Lord, I wait for God my Saviour; my God will hear me. Do not gloat over me, my enemy! Though I have fallen, I will rise.

This statement has to be seen in the context of the passage we have just been studying. Micah had been describing stages in the corruption of society that he saw in Jerusalem. His description reached the stage where all relationships were corrupted, even marriage as the most intimate human relationship – no one and nothing could be trusted.

When trust breaks down all human interaction is affected. No one's word can be trusted and the structure of society begins to crumble. Business deals are not honoured, national pacts and treaties are not to be trusted, followed by suspicion, conflict, war, destruction, and international disaster.

Micah's message of warning is highly relevant today with rising levels of young people addicted to mobile phones where they absorb false news, conspiracy theories, lies and deceit. This comes at a time when the yardstick of truth from biblical teaching is no longer readily available in family life or in school for most children.

This was what Micah was seeing in Jerusalem where the teaching of truth in the Torah had been neglected for generations. Idolatry, false gods, lies and deception in public life were leading towards national disaster. He could clearly foresee what actually did happen about 40 years later.

"A man's enemies are members of his own household" he said, indicating that corruption had now reached the zenith of penetration into all levels of society. It was at this point that he could do no other than throw himself upon the mercy of God. *"As for me, I watch in hope for the Lord. I wait for God my Saviour."*

There was no hope, unless God intervened to save the nation, as he had done in the time of his predecessor Isaiah when the Assyrians were laying siege to Jerusalem, and Isaiah and King Hezekiah had prayed together (Is 37:36). Micah had given the clearest warning that he could sound. There was nothing more he could do. He could only watch and hope that God would do something.

Micah also knew that God is a God of justice as well as love and mercy. He knew that God **could** intervene. But was this in the best interests of the nation? Micah, at this point, may have been foreseeing that God would work out his good purposes for the nation through a remnant in exile in Babylon through Ezekiel's leadership. They would reach the point of full repentance – where they actually loathed themselves (Ezek 36.31). It was after that point had been reached that God gave Ezekiel the vision of the new Jerusalem. This was what Micah was looking for when he said, *"Though I have fallen, I will rise. Though I sit in darkness, the Lord will be my light."*

Micah's confidence was not in his own quality of faith, but in his understanding of the purposes of God, or the ways of the Lord – ***using death and resurrection***. Ezekiel had also come to this understanding of the ways of God. He knew that there had to be full repentance before the love and mercy of God would change the whole situation. There had to be a death to the old ways of humanity, before there could be new ways of living as the people of God.

Micah had already reached this understanding of God's nature and purposes, but he did not just sit and wait, he actively acknowledged his own sinfulness, *"Because I have sinned against him I will bear the Lord's wrath, until he pleads my case and establishes my right. He will bring me out into the light."*

Micah knew that there are inevitable consequences of human sin. We all have to bear those consequences of our own unrighteous actions – and so, collectively, do nations. But Micah knew that God was longing to change the whole situation as soon as there was a glimmer of repentance. Jeremiah knew this truth which is why he was able to declare God's word, *"If at any time I announce that a nation or kingdom is to be uprooted, torn down and destroyed, and if that nation I warned repents of its evil, then I will relent and not inflict on it the disaster I had planned"* (Jer 18:7-8). Jesus taught exactly the same message in his parable of the prodigal son whose father rushed to embrace him as soon as he repented (Lk 15:11f). It is only God who is the hope of the world!

21 THE LIGHT OF THE WORLD   Micah 7:10-13

Then my enemy will see it and will be covered with shame, she who said to me, "Where is the Lord your God?" My eyes will see her downfall; even now she will be trampled underfoot like mire in the streets.

The starting point of this passage is in the last statement of verse 9. *"He will bring me out* (Hebrew *yotsieni*) *into the light; I will see his righteousness."* The Hebrew word *yatsa* is the verb 'to bring out' that is often used for the 'Exodus', when God brought his people out of the darkness of slavery into the light of his presence at Mount Sinai. This indicates what Micah was trying to convey – that God would do something like a 'new exodus' to rescue his people from the darkness that was coming as a result of their sinfulness. In his love and mercy, as he had responded to their cries in Egypt, he would once again rescue the nation **after her downfall.** The enemies of Israel would see the transformation of Israel's fortunes that God would accomplish.

Micah does not say that there will be no darkness – quite the opposite! Jerusalem was going to have to bear the wrath of the Lord, but God's act of redemption would be a witness to the enemy. Those who scoffed saying, *"Where is the Lord your God?"* would be shamed. Micah probably had in mind the time when Isaiah and Hezekiah went into the temple with the letter from Sennacherib saying, *"Do not let the God you depend on deceive you when he says, Jerusalem will not be handed over to the king of Assyria"* (Is 37:10). This had happened in Micah's lifetime. He would have remembered the incident from his boyhood when God answered prayer by destroying the Assyrian invaders and he was referring to this saying the enemy would be trampled underfoot and he would see her downfall.

Micah referred to the day for building walls; not *rebuilding* the walls but **building new walls** in the day for extending the boundaries of the land. He foresaw a time of renewal and prosperity for Israel. Their enemies would be shamed. Those who said, *"Where is your God?"* would see the transformation that God would bring to Israel. The importance of this was not to elevate Israel, but to demonstrate